BEIJING

GW00402083

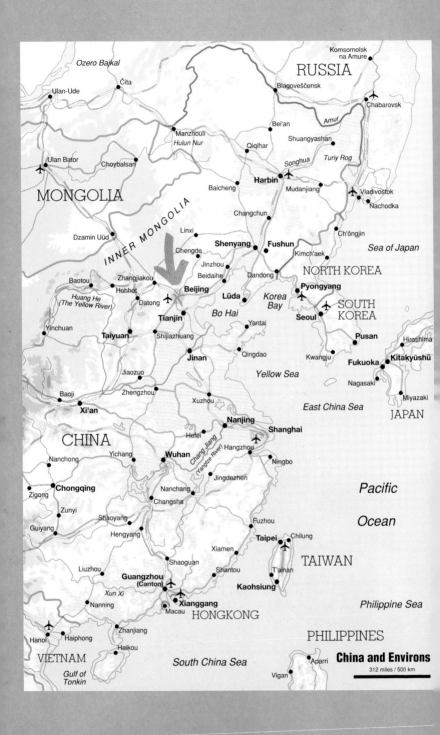

China and Environs

312 miles / 500 km

Dear Visitor!

Beijing is all about grandiosity – the Great Wall, the Forbidden City, Tiananmen Square and the Temple of Heaven. It is, after all, the capital for one quarter of the world's population. Every ruler, for hundreds of years, has molded the city in his own image, creating layer upon layer of architectural statements. But Beijing is also a village that creeps between and sprawls beyond the halls of power. In the alleyways of the city, life comprises a myriad of wonderful little traditions – like raising crickets, flying kites and riding bicycles.

 Kari Huus, our correspondent, has seen the many faces of Beijing in her four years in the city, as a reporter for Newsweek magazine and an avid explorer of the city's backstreets. She arrived in the aftermath of the 1989 Tiananmen movement and was present throughout the last dramatic wave of economic reform. 'It feels like I've been living in several different places at the same time. The mood and the landscape of the city keep changing,' she says, 'depending on your vantage point.' A fluent speaker of Mandarin, Huus knows people as diverse as communist officials, playwrights and bicycle repairmen.

Huus brings a keen insight and enthusiasm to this book, filled with details that bring this historically rich and quirky capital to life. Her day itineraries include all the major highlights while the shorter tours take in a variety of historical sites, temples, parks and as many of her favourite markets and alleyways as she can squeeze in. She's also created two excursions – to Bedaihe beach, where China's top brass hobnob and Chengde, a cluster of Buddhist temples in the mountains. Her carefully-devised itineraries anticipate the vagaries of travel in China and offer good old-fashioned advice on how to cope. As the Chinese say, 'Yilupingan' – Happy Trails!

Hans Höfer
Publisher, Insight Guides

C O N T E N T S

Pages 2/3:
the mammoth
Tiananmen Square

Excursions

*Pages 10/11:
the highly-stylized
Peking Opera in action*

Shopping, Dining & Nightlife

Calendar of Events

Practical Information

Maps

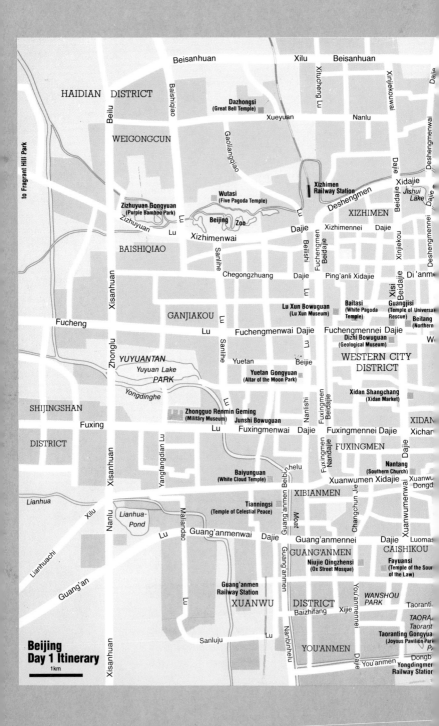

Beijing
Day 1 Itinerary
1km

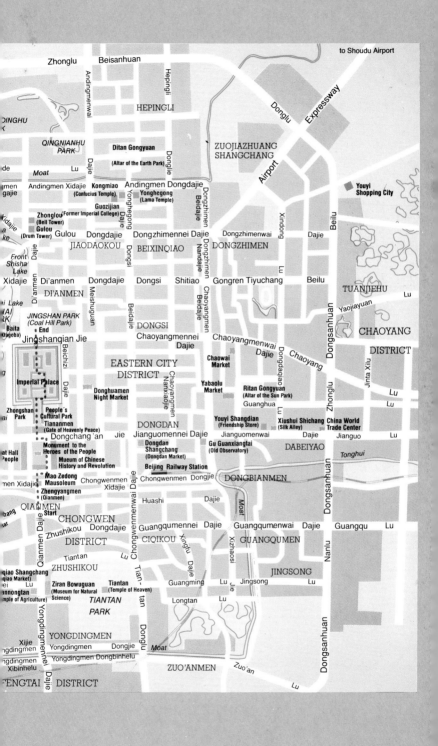

to Shoudu Airport

Zhonglu   Beisanhuan

HEPINGLI

QINGNIANHU
PARK

Ditan Gongyuan
(Altar of the Earth Park)

ZUOJIAZHUANG
SHANGCHANG

Moat

Andingmen Xidajie   Kongmiao   Andingmen Dongdajie
                     (Confucius Temple)

                     Guozijian   Yonghegong
Zhonglou   (Former Imperial College) (Lama Temple)
(Bell Tower)

Gulou   Gulou Dongdajie   Dongzhimennei Dajie   DONGZHIMEN
(Drum Tower)

JIAODAOKOU   BEIXINQIAO   Dongzhimenwai

Youyi
Shopping City

Front
Shisha
Lake

Xidajie   Di'anmen   Dongdajie   Dongsi   Shitiao   Gongren Tiyuchang   Beilu   TUANJIEHU
                                                                                                            Lu
         DI'ANMEN

JINGSHAN PARK   Yaojiayuan
(Coal Hill Park)   CHAOYANG
Baita   DONGSI   DISTRICT
(Dagoba)   End
Jingshanqian Jie   Chaoyangmennei   Chaoyangmenwai
                          Dajie   Dajie   Chaoyang

EASTERN CITY   Chaowai
DISTRICT   Market

Imperial Palace   Yabaolu
                 Donghuamen   Market   Ritan Gongyuan
Zhongshan   Night Market   (Altar of the Sun Park)
Park   People's   Guanghua
       Cultural Park
       Tiananmen   DONGDAN   Youyi Shangdian   Xiushui Shichang China World
       (Gate of Heavenly Peace)   (Friendship Store)   (Silk Alley)   Trade Center
       Dongchang'an   Jie   Jianguomennei Dajie   Jianguomenwai   Dajie   Jianguo   Lu
       Monument to the
       Heroes of the People   Dongdan   Gu Guanxiangtai   DABEIYAO
       Museum of Chinese   Shangchang   (Old Observatory)   Tonghui
       History and Revolution   (Dongdan Market)
       Mao Zedong   Beijing Railway Station
       Mausoleum
men Xidajie Chongwenmen   Chongwenmen Dongjie   DONGBIANMEN
             Xidajie
       Zhengyangmen
       (Qianmen)   Huashi   Dajie

QIANMEN
       Start
CHONGWEN   Guangqumennei   Dajie   Guangqumenwai   Dajie   Guangqu   Lu
       Zhushikou Dongdajie   CIQIKOU   GUANGQUMEN
DISTRICT
       Tiantan   JINGSONG
qiao Shangchang Lu   Guangming   Lu   Jingsong   Lu
(qiao Market)   Tiantan
ZHUSHIKOU   (Temple of Heaven)
nnongtan   Ziran Bowuguan   TIANTAN   Longtan   Lu
mple of Agriculture) (Museum for Natural PARK
           Science)

YONGDINGMEN
       Yongdingmen   Dongjie
   Xijie   Moat
ngdingmen
ngdingmen   Yongdingmen Dongbinhelu   ZUO'ANMEN
Xibinhelu
FENGTAI DISTRICT

HISTORY

Mao Zedong's historic address

The well-worn image of Chairman Mao, standing on the gate to the Imperial City and proclaiming the founding of the People's Republic of China is symbolic of Beijing's importance as the capital of this vast country. But the city's rise has been violent and uncertain. Only after many cycles of destruction and reconstruction has the garrison town become the political and cultural centre of the Middle Kingdom.

Frontier Days

The discovery of the Peking Man in 1929 proves that settlements of some kind existed here up to 500,000 years ago. In recorded history, however, Beijing goes back to about 1000BC, when it was a trading town called Jicheng (City of Reeds). Because of its strategic location on the edge of the agrarian plains to the south and the steppes to the north, it became a garrison town, changing hands repeatedly as kingdoms in the north fought their turf wars.

Qin Shi Huangdi, the first emperor of the Qin dynasty, unified China in 221BC, making Beijing part of one of the world's largest empires of the day. This same ruler later became obsessed with protecting China's northern frontier, by connecting walls built by previous kingdoms to form the Great Wall. The grandiose project was continued by successive rulers, but the city was still overrun and ruled as often by northern tribes.

Culture

Mongol Conquest and Rule (1276–1368)

When Genghis Khan's armies swept across the northern plains and stormed Beijing in 1215, the month-long invasion was the most brutal suffered by the area. The court's treasures were looted and the city razed to the ground. But from these ashes rose one of the world's greatest capitals.

By 1279, Genghis Khan's grandson, Kublai Khan ruled not only all of China, but over much of the Eurasian continental mass, from Annam (Vietnam) to the Baltic Sea. But, like other foreign rulers before and after him, he was as much conquered by China as it was by him. He built his capital at the present site of Beijing and named it *Dadu* (Great Capital), though it is better known by its Mongolian name, *Khan Balik* (City of Khan).

Kublai Khan

Kublai Khan was charmed by Buddhism and interested in China's advanced astronomy and farming methods. For lack of educated Mongol officials, his administrators were mostly Chinese and his capital, a copy of traditional Chinese cities.

This was the city that impressed Marco Polo. The Italian merchant, fresh from medieval Europe, noted that *Dadu* was laid out with the precision of a chessboard, with broad, straight streets lined with fine courtyard homes and inns. There were hostels in the suburbs for merchants from all over the known world, amply served by some 20,000 prostitutes. And in the city centre, where Beihai is today, stood the Great Khan's palace, surrounded by a 6½-km (4-mile) long wall.

Like those in the previous dynasties, the later generations of officials became increasingly corrupt and inept. The Mongols exported much of China's wealth to other parts of their kingdom and

Construction of the Forbidden City began under Emperor Yongle

starvation was widespread. A peasant uprising in 1368 overthrew Kublai Khan's descendants easily, ending Mongolian rule in China.

The Ming Dynasty

With the founding of the Ming Dynasty (1368–1644), the Chinese were again masters of a unified China. Logically enough, the new rulers moved their capital to Nanjing, in the heart of a rich agricultural region near the mouth of the Yangtze River. With an eye to expanding China's northern territory, Emperor Yongle later moved the capital back north, calling it Beijing (Northern Capital).

Emperor Yongle's reign (1403–25), at the beginning of the Ming Dynasty, was Imperial Beijing's cultural pinnacle, particularly in terms of architecture. The Forbidden City that now stands, with its sweeping yellow tiled roofs, was constructed under Yongle and has remained symbolic of Beijing's pre-eminence ever since. Tiananmen (Gate of Heavenly Peace), now adorned with Mao's smiling portrait, is a legacy of that period. So is the city's most striking structure, the Temple of Heaven, where the emperor communed with the gods twice yearly. Yongle also rebuilt Kublai Khan's city walls around the imperial city and added another rectangle encompassing the Temple of Heaven in the south.

Soon after Yongle's death, however, China closed itself to the outside world and forbade its people to emigrate or explore foreign lands. Foreigners were, by and large, despised for their barbarian ways. So, too, the Chinese rejected Western science, which had just begun to revolutionize the outside world. This paranoia and insecurity led to a retardation of China's growth in areas such as astronomy and navigation, where it had once been a frontrunner.

Each successive emperor also became increasingly caught up in palace ceremony and isolated from the world outside. Palace eunuchs became corrupt and powerful, siphoning riches from the palace and forcing heavy taxes on the poor. They controlled information to the emperor so that news of peasant rebellions did not always reach him. Not surprisingly, a peasant rebellion easily toppled the Ming dynasty in 1644 and paved the way for the Manchus' invasion 43 days later.

The Qing Dynasty

Unlike the invaders before them, the Manchus who founded the Qing dynasty (1644–1911) did not destroy the city they occupied. Prolific builders and renovators, the Qing rulers built lavish palaces for themselves, mixing the styles of past dynasties, often with gaudy results. Under their care, many of the 800 or so pavilions, palaces and temples built by the Ming were kept in fair condition at the turn of the 20th century. Today, most of the relics in Beijing date to the 600 years of Ming and Qing rule.

The Qing dynasty emperors tried to grapple with the problems that had toppled the Ming. They preserved the Chinese examination system for choosing officials, slashed the number of eunuchs to minimize court intrigue and tried to reform the tax system. By far the most colourful character was Qianlong (1736–99), the longest reigning Chinese emperor. Qianlong was a despot who ruthlessly suppressed intellectuals whom he suspected of disloyalty. But he was also a lover of the arts and responsible for some of the more flamboyant architectural details in the city. Under his rule, Chinese territory expanded dramatically northwards and westwards. By the end of the 1800s, Beijing ruled over four times as much territory as during the Ming dynasty.

The Fall

While China expanded in the 1700s, Western colonial powers and foreign trade were changing the face of the globe. Beijing became increasingly suspicious of the outside world. Foreign trade was limited to Canton and frustrated by complex regulations. The British, who wanted greater

Old Beijing

access to the Chinese market, sent a high level delegation aboard a man-of-war loaded with expensive gifts and state-of-the-art technology in 1793 to the Chinese port of Tianjin. But Emperor Qianlong rebuffed the British with an edict to King George III, stating that China did not need to trade with Britain because she 'already possessed everything a civilized people could ever want'. Britain's request to set up a consulate in Beijing was also rejected.

Puyi, last emperor of China

But Britain had a growing trade deficit with China and would not take no for an answer. Backed by military force, foreign traders pressed shipments of opium on the Chinese market to offset their growing trade deficit. The First Opium War of 1840 forced the palace to allow foreign governments extra-territoriality in an area just outside the palace gates. By the end of the Second Opium War in 1860, the Qing emperor had fled to Chengde while Western troops destroyed a large swathe of the city, including the old Summer Palace. The rulers' impotence infuriated the Chinese. Secret societies sprang up and small-scale rebellions became common.

In the final days of the Qing Dynasty, the palace was a fortress against the reality of China's decay and the stage where the last court tragedy was acted out. The emperor's favourite concubine, Cixi, rose to eminence after a power struggle in the palace in 1861. Empress Cixi dominated and terrorized the court, but she could not hold the crumbling kingdom together. In 1900, a secret society called the Boxers laid siege to the foreign legation quarter for 50 days and Cixi was forced to flee. Before her death in 1908, she installed three-year-old Puyi on the throne. His story is powerfully told in the 1988 movie, *The Last Emperor*.

The Republican Era

In 1911, a revolution led by Dr Sun Yat-sen attempted to launch China into the modern world. It ended imperial rule, but the age-old problems of feuding warlords, poverty and factionalism continued for another 30 years.

At the end of World War I, Western powers continued to carve up China for themselves. The Versailles Treaty ceded Chinese territory to the Japanese, humiliating China. The reaction to this marked a turning point in the Chinese people's psyche: students and intellectuals around the country took to the streets in a revolution that came to be known as the May Fourth Movement of 1919, demanding independence and territorial integrity.

In 1927, the Nationalist Party (Kuomingtang) tried to unify China again by force. On 10 October 1928, it formally founded the Republic of China with its capital in Nanjing. In the countryside,

Red Guards waving Mao's Red Book of quotations

the Chinese Communist Party (CCP), founded in Shanghai in 1921 and led by a young Mao Zedong, waged a guerrilla war against the new government. But the Japanese occupation of China soon forced the Nationalists and the Communists to form an uneasy alliance. This only lasted until the end of World War II. In the bitter civil war that followed, the Communists had the final word.

Communist China

In true imperial style, Mao Zedong declared the founding of the People's Republic of China (PRC) from the reviewing stand of Tiananmen, restoring Beijing as the capital in 1949. The new regime took to their task with the zeal of a mop-up task force. They redistributed land to the peasants (killing many in the former ruling classes in the process) and undertook massive industrialization projects. In Beijing, slums were razed, new Soviet-style factories and buildings built, streets widened and transportation improved. New universities were also built. In 1957, most of the city walls were demolished as were hundreds of temples and historical sites. Twelve thousand 'volunteers' worked at breakneck speed to complete Tiananmen Square and the gargantuan buildings surrounding it in time for the PRC's 10th anniversary.

But the euphoria was followed by a series of political campaigns which left deep scars on the whole nation. The anti-Rightist movement of 1957 targeted intellectuals, capitalists and other 'class enemies'. Hot on its heels was the Great Leap Forward (1958–60), a disastrous attempt to modernize the country overnight.

The most devastating mass movement was the Cultural Revolution (1966–76) during which millions of young Chinese were encouraged to wage war on feudal and bourgeois culture. The truth, which became clear after Mao's death in 1976, was a disgraceful reminder of dynastic rule: the Gang of Four, headed by Mao's wife were using the movement to gain power as Mao's health declined.

The 'class war', which lasted for a decade, left thousands of historical relics defaced or destroyed and caused appalling loss of life and near economic collapse. The death of Premier Zhou Enlai (regarded as a moderating force in the government) in January 1976 sparked mass mourning in Beijing, which turned into an anguished outcry for change.

Reform Years

Since Mao's death in September 1976 and the disgrace of the Gang of Four, Beijing has been struggling to modernize and lead the rest of China along the path of progress. Ideology has gradually been discarded for economic reform under Deng Xiaoping's leadership since 1978. Chinese people today have more contact with the outside world. The rigid state bureaucracy is also giving way to a more freewheeling society.

But these new policies involve a balancing act, and nowhere is it clearer than in Beijing: in 1979, the Democracy Wall Movement brought millions onto the streets, calling for greater political freedom. In 1986, a democratic movement in the central Chinese city of Hefei soon sparked off protests in Beijing and Shanghai. Both events, led by students and intellectuals, were followed by repression of the press, arts and political reformers. In 1989, millions of students and workers marched to Tiananmen Square to appeal for political reform. When the military moved in to quell the demonstrators on 4 June, a pall of silence fell over the city.

While martial law troops lined the Avenue of Eternal Peace, Beijing's future seemed bleak. Political reform was not in the offing and economic reform seemed threatened. But after some political jockeying, senior leader Deng Xiaoping made a highly publicized tour to the booming southern provinces in 1992 where his reforms had taken hold. Deng's brainchild – the socialist market economy – became the core of party and government policy by March 1993. Deng's logic was simple: if people became rich, the rest would take care of itself.

New Beijing

Perhaps no place in China has changed more dramatically in the 1990s than Beijing. Every day, more people abandon government jobs for the cellular phones of entrepreneurship. McDonald's and MTV have made their entry. Accounting is replacing Marxist studies in universities and the arts are emerging. Frenzied construction of new roads, hotels and shopping centres is underway, and temples and towers are being renovated. There is a sense of expectation that Beijing will become the nucleus of a powerful empire. For the traveller, there is no time like the present to see the city at the crossroads between the past and the future.

18

Historical Highlights

1030–221BC The city of Ji develops at the site of Beijing.

221–207BC Qin Shi Huangdi unifies China and begins building the Great Wall.

200BC–AD1200 Beijing becomes a strategic garrison town between warring kingdoms.

1215 Mongols led by Genghis Khan overrun Beijing.

1260 Kublai Khan founds the Mongol (Yuan) dynasty.

1271 Kublai Khan establishes the capital of Dadu or Khan Balik at Beijing's site. Marco Polo visits China.

1368–1644 The Ming dynasty.

1400s Forbidden City and most of the existing Great Wall built.

1644–1911 Manchu or Qing dynasty is established.

1839–42 First Opium War forces open five Chinese ports.

1860 The Second Opium War.

1861–1908 Cixi rises to power.

1900 Boxer Uprising lays seige to the Foreign Legation Quarter.

1911 Revolution headed by Sun Yat-sen ends dynastic rule.

1919 May 4th Movement for democracy and sovereignty is sparked off by the Versailles Treaty.

1921 China's Communist Party is founded in Shanghai.

1928 Republican government establishes its capital in Nanjing.

1935 Communists embark on the Long March to escape from Nationalist forces.

1937 The Marco Polo Bridge Incident sets off a full-scale invasion by the Japanese, who occupy China until the end of World War II.

1949 Mao Zedong declares the founding of the People's Republic of China. Beijing becomes the capital.

1957–59 Tiananmen Square and surrounding monoliths are built. Most of the city wall is demolished.

1957 The Hundred Flowers Movement launched by Mao urges intellectual expression.

1957 The Anti-Rightist Movement singles out at least 300,000 intellectuals for criticism, punishment or imprisonment.

1958 Mao launches the Great Leap Forward.

1959–62 Famine claims the lives of 20 million people.

1960 Beijing and Moscow split over ideology, followed by two decades of Cold War.

1966–76 Cultural Revolution. Widespread persecution, chaos and near economic collapse occurs.

1972 US President Richard Nixon visits Beijing, marking the first official contact between the US and the PRC.

1976 Deaths of Premier Zhou Enlai and Chairman Mao Zedong. The Gang of Four tries to seize power but is later arrested.

1978 Deng Xiaoping launches economic reforms.

1979 Democracy Wall Movement is quashed.

1980 Gang of Four is tried on nationwide television. Economic and political reforms are effected.

1989 Soviet President Mikhail Gorbachev visits Beijing.

1989 Democracy Movement is crushed by China's military.

1990 Beijing hosts the 11th Asian Games, marking its return to the international community.

1992 Deng Xiaoping tours southern cities. Japanese Emperor Akihito visits China. The first McDonald's opens near Tiananmen Square.

1993 China's Parliament officially endorses market economy.

1994 Structural reforms of financial, currency and taxation systems mark dramatic push towards market economy.

Beijing is the capital and political nerve centre of China, but it is far from the geographical centre. Located on the northern plain about 180km (112 miles) from the ocean, it suffers bitter winters, blistering summers and ferocious winds. The good news is that Beijing, with 11 million inhabitants, is not as crowded as other major southern and coastal cities.

Beijing municipality covers 16,808sq km (6,488sq miles), so sightseeing entails covering a lot of ground. The three *Day Itineraries* that follow cover the Forbidden City in central Beijing, the Summer Palace in the northwest edge and the Great Wall in the outlying counties to the north.

Central Beijing

The city is laid out on a grid, with Chang'an Avenue (Avenue of Eternal Peace) dividing the city into the north and south sections. Street names change according to their relationship with the gates in the former city wall. Chang'an Avenue, for example, turns into Fuxing-mennei which means 'inside Fuxing Gate' to the west and Fuxingmenwai or 'outside Fuxing Gate' further west. Three ring roads loop around the city.

Taxis are the best mode of transport. They are abundant and reasonably priced, especially the mini-vans or 'bread loaf cars'. The subway is all right for getting to the general vicinity of your destination, and buses can be recommended in a few cases. Bicycles are a good way to see the city and can be rented at many hotels.

After taking in the big ticket items, begin roaming Beijing's maze of *hutongs* (alleyways). The *Pick & Mix* itineraries are punctuated with visits to temples, parks and museums, but will also lead you through interesting neighbourhoods, markets and happenings on stage. By big city standards, Beijing is remarkably safe, friendly and inexpensive. So fear not. Take the following suggestions as a jump-off point for your own exploration of the city.

DAY (1)

Tiananmen Square, Forbidden City and Jingshan Park

A front door to back door trek through the imperial heart of the city, leading through Tiananmen Square, the palace and the gardens of Jingshan Park.

– Take the subway to Qianmen stop and exit on the north. Bus Nos 17, 47 and 212 also stop here. There are two gate towers referred to as Zhengyangmen; go to the north one on the square –

A first day of exploring Beijing starts logically enough at the front gate or **Qianmen** (also called **Zhengyangmen**). This tower (open daily 8.30am–5pm) is the largest of nine similar gates in the wall

that used to embrace the Inner City, and at its centre, the palace or Forbidden City. Zhengyangmen, built here in 1419, was destroyed during the Boxer Rebellion of 1900 and rebuilt in 1905. The gate provides a great vantage point for seeing the layout of old Beijing.

Looking out south from Zhengyangmen's observation platform, directly across the street is a companion gate which served as a watchtower against invasion. This was built in 1439. The Outer City, which was also enclosed by a high

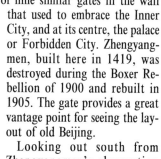

Posing at Zhengyangmen gate

wall, extends southward. The bustling narrow streets to the south are Dashalar, a district which at the turn of the century was alive with decadent pleasures for off-duty officials (see *Pick & Mix 5*). Beyond it is the Temple of Heaven.

The north side of the tower overlooks Tiananmen Square, in the middle of which stands an obelisk. On the left stands the Great Hall of the People and on the right is the imposing Museum of Chinese History and Revolution. Dead centre is the Mao Zedong Mausoleum.

At the far end of the square, across Chang'an Avenue is Tiananmen, the Gate of Heavenly Peace. Beyond is the Forbidden City, or Imperial Palace, now officially called the Palace Museum. Just to the west of the palace is Zhongshan Park, dedicated to the memory of Republican leader Dr Sun Yat-sen. It used to be part of the palace, as did Zhongnanhai, just a little further to the west, where China's top leaders live. To the northwest, you'll easily spot a white stupa. This marks Beihai Park, once part of the imperial gardens.

Centre of the Square

Before leaving Zhengyangmen, be sure to visit the photo exhibition inside. It gives a wonderful view of Beijing at the turn of the century, from cricket fighting and geomancers to camel caravans arriving at the city gate.

Next, pay respects at the **Mao Zedong Mausoleum** (open daily 8.30am–11.30am; Monday, Wednesday and Friday 2–4pm). This was built after Mao's death in 1976 and remains a standard feature for Chinese travellers and grade school outings. There is no entrance fee, but you must leave your bag at the door. The queue may appear long but visitors are hustled past Mao's crystal sarcophagus briskly, so the tour doesn't take that long.

Statuary at Mao Zedong Mausoleum

The 37-m (121-ft) high obelisk in the centre of the square that you saw earlier is called the **Monument to the Heroes of the People**, dedicated in 1958 to those who died for the country. The bas relief on the pedestal portrays the struggle from the First Opium War in 1840 to the founding of the PRC in 1949. Start on the east side and move clockwise to see it chronologically.

Next, visit the **Great Hall of the People** (Monday–Saturday, 8.30am–3pm) where China's parliament convenes every March and where the Communist Party holds its congress. There is a brief tour which will give you a basic idea. If you're feeling very ambitious, cross the square to the monolith housing the **Museum of Chinese History and Revolution** (open daily 8.30am–5pm, except Monday). One of the most blatantly Stalinist structures in the city, it was completed in 1959 and opened to the public in 1961. Supported by 11 columns, a vast entrance hall connects two wings.

Excursion to Great Hall of the People

In the left wing, the displays chronicle the evolution of the Communist Party from the May 4th Movement of 1919. In the right wing, Chinese history from the Peking Man (500,000BC) to the Sui Dynasty (AD581–618) is covered. Exhibits on the third floor cover the period from the Tang Dynasty to 1919.

Since the interpretation of history is politically problematic, the museum was closed for most of the Cultural Revolution. In 1989, it was closed again during the pro-democracy demonstrations when soldiers occupied it. Its subsequent renovation was delayed by lack of finance and the museum is expected to re-open at time of press.

Relax awhile in **Tiananmen Square**. In imperial times, two rows of ministry offices for the Ming and Qing governments stood at its site. When the emperor wanted to hand down an edict, he would pass with great fanfare to deliver it to the Ministry of Rites, where it was recopied and sent throughout the empire. Tiananmen Square, along with the museum and the Great Hall were built in record time – just 10 months between 1958 and 1959 by some 12,000 workers working overtime.

Tiananmen dwarfs all other public squares, including Moscow's Red Square. The Tiananmen area has been the stage for anti-government demonstrations, mass rallies and parades both before and since the building of the square. On a normal day, it's just a convenient place to gather and show off one's best home-made kite. Before moving on to the Forbidden City, grab a pedicab to the **Beijing Hotel** (33, East Chang'an Avenue) for lunch. Try the *gongbao* chicken with red-hot chillies and peanuts at the moderately-priced **Sichuan**

Tiananmen Gate

Restaurant (open daily 11am–2pm, 4.30–7.30pm) in the old section. Or go to one of the little Mongolian hotpot restaurants down in the Qianmen alleys, distinguishable from the other eateries by the outline of a pot in the window.

Enter the **Imperial City** at **Tiananmen Gate**, where China's revolutionary and feudal legacies converge. The gate, built in 1417 and restored in 1651, is anachronistically adorned with a portrait of Mao Zedong and two slogans: 'Long Live the People's Republic of China' and 'Long Live the Great Union of the Peoples of the World'. This was where Mao announced the founding of the PRC before a crowd of 300,000 people. Of the five gates and five matching marble bridges, only the emperor could use the middle one.

From Tiananmen Gate there is a long approach, leading through a second gate, before you reach the **Forbidden City** or **Palace Museum** (open daily 8.30am–4.30pm; tickets for foreigners are sold at the kiosk on the far right). Enter the Forbidden City through the glass doors on the right where you will be offered, free of charge, a cassette tape 'acoustiguide' tour in any one of eight languages. I highly recommend the 45-minute-long tape; it offers the best of palace stories and you can always turn it off if you want to linger at a particular site. It also muffles the sound of other sightseers so you can appreciate the palace in peace.

The palace construction began under Ming Emperor Yongle in 1407. It took 200,000 workers and 13 years to complete, but it proved to be a durable home for 24 emperors throughout the rule of the Ming (1368–1644) and Qing (1644–1911) dynasties. Though parts have been damaged and rebuilt, the basic structure has changed little. No foreigners or commoners were allowed beyond the main gate, **Wumen**, without special permission until after the fall of the Qing, and few were tempted to charge this massive three-sided tower. The emperor would review his armies from the viewing stand on top, and prisoners were paraded past him so he could decide whom to pardon and whom to execute.

The palace forms an enormous rectangle, 101ha (250 acres) in area, surrounded

Hall of Heavenly Purity, Palace Museum

by a moat nearly 50m (164ft) wide and with 10-m (33-ft) high walls. It is divided into front and rear sections. In the front are three public halls where the emperors held important ceremonies. The rear part of the complex is made up of three main palaces and some smaller quarters to either side, where the rulers and their concubines and families lived. The only adult male in the palace was the emperor, surrounded by concubines, eunuchs, the empress, female servants and slaves.

It's easy to see how the emperors became isolated from the goings-on in the kingdom. The imperial rulers and their families rarely, if ever, left the palace. The last emperor, Puyi, and the vestiges of royal court lived in the rear palaces well into the Republican era. Finally in 1925, Puyi left the palace and in 1932 became the nominal emperor of Manchuguo, under the control of the Japanese. Though many of the palace treasures were stolen by Japanese invaders or carted off to Taiwan by the Nationalists towards the end of the civil war, there is still an impressive collection of gilded *objets d'art*.

The absolute power of the emperor is reflected in every aspect of the palace design, down to the most minute detail. The halls are built along a central axis, each with three gates. The central one was always reserved for the sedan chair of the emperor. Each ramp, over which the emperor was carried to the gates of each hall, has dragons – the symbol of imperial majesty – carved in stone. There are thousands of dragon head drains and hundreds of thousands of dragons painted into the ornate ceilings of the palace.

There are many architectural details in the palace which you'll often see in Chinese imperial architecture. For example, on the eaves of nearly every roof are a parade of little creatures, often led by a man riding on a hen's back. These creatures were thought to discourage lightning from striking. The man on the hen, according to another theory, represents a tyrannical prince who was hung from the roof beam to discourage threats to the emperor. Another

A female lion with its cub

mystery are the 'lions' that stand guard at gates throughout China. On the right, you'll often find a male lion with a ball – thought to represent the world – under his paw. On the left is the female, with a cub under her paw. But since there were no lions in China as far as natural historians know, the gate lions probably represent some other animal or come from legend. They have come to symbolize strength and dignity.

Colours and multiples of things have symbolic meaning too. The yellow of the palace roof tiles represent the Earth, while the red of the walls stand for fire, luck and happiness. Blue and green are for spring and rebirth. Nine is a lucky number. Count the dragons on the ramps to the halls and the gold nubs on the doors. The acoustiguide tour leads you to the rear gate, **Shenwumen**, north of the Forbidden City, where you can drop off your tape recorder.

On both sides of the street, **Jingshanqian Jie**, are food vendors. Buy a Xinjiang-style mutton kebab and sit for a spell before exploring **Jingshan Park** (open daily 6am–9pm), directly across. Also known as **Coal Hill Park**, Jingshan was the private garden of the emperor as early as the Yuan Dynasty. The hill – the highest point in the city before the advent of highrise buildings – was built from soil removed during the digging of the palace moat during the Ming Dynasty. From the **Ten Thousand Springs Pavilion** at its summit, you get a terrific overview of the palace roofs at dusk.

In Emperor Qianlong's day, the park was stocked with deer, hares, rabbits and thousands of songbirds. Today, love birds occupy every park bench in this quiet garden. On the north side of the park is the spot where a Ming emperor hung himself. A tree has been replanted and marked for dramatic effect. For dinner, try **Dasanyuan** restaurant (open daily 4.30–7pm; Tel: 440-218) which serves Cantonese food. Turn right as you leave Jingshan Park and walk 200m (220yds) to the corner to get there.

DAY 2

Fragrant Hills Park, Summer Palace and Sakler Gallery

Takes in the Fragrant Hills Park, the Summer Palace and Sakler Gallery in northwest Beijing, where emperors and poets retreated from the summer heat.

– The Fragrant Hills lie 28km (17½ miles) northwest of the city. Allow one hour for a taxi ride from central Beijing. Or take the public bus (Nos 7, 15, 19, 27 and 45) from your hotel, connecting with bus No 360 at the Beijing Zoo. It takes at least 90 minutes from the city centre, plus a 15-minute walk up the park entrance from the bus terminus to get there. The tour easily takes nine hours from 8am–5pm. Wear walking shoes and get an early start. If weather permits, this would be a good opportunity for a picnic lunch –

From the 12th century until about 300 years ago, **Fragrant Hills Park** or **Xiangshan Gongyuan** was a favourite hunting retreat for the emperors, many of whom made their mark by building pagodas and temples here. At its height, under the Qing Dynasty emperor Qianlong, the park had a wall around it and was stocked with exotic deer. Much of the park fell into decay or was destroyed by European armies in 1860 and 1900, but it is gradually being restored.

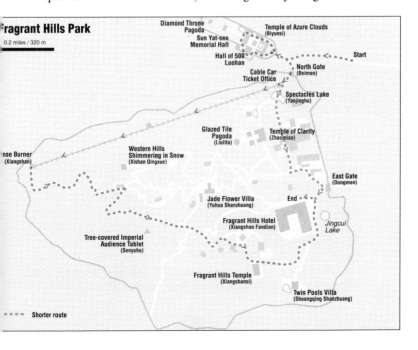

The ticket office is just left of the main entrance. Once inside, follow the stone path that veers right and buy another ticket to visit the **Temple of the Azure Clouds**, or **Biyunsi** (open daily 8.30am–4pm) first.

A temple was first built on this hillside in 1330 and buildings were added over the centuries, largely during the Qing Dynasty. In the lower courtyards, you'll come across several halls with good examples of Buddhist images seen all over China. The first hall contains two very large celestial guardians, and the second a statue of Maitreya Buddha, both dating to the Ming Dynasty. The innermost hall has been turned into the **Sun Yat-sen Memorial Hall**, in memory of the founder of the Nationalist Party that replaced the last dynasty. To the right of his statue is a crystal coffin, a gift from the Soviet Union for the revolutionary leader's body. It was never used because the Chinese had made other funeral arrangements.

What sets this temple apart from many others is the Indian-style white marble **Diamond Throne Pagoda** towering high above the trees at the rear of the complex. On the first level you'll find a sanctuary carved with monster heads – the design of which can be traced back to China's earliest societies. The sanctuary, which is now walled shut, held Sun Yat-sen's body from 1925 to 1929, before it was moved to Nanjing. Climb up the inner stairways and you'll find yourself on the top terrace with a tall central tower surrounded by six small pagodas, all smothered with delicately-carved *bodhisattvas* (enlightened beings).

Diamond Throne Pagoda detail

As you're descending, just after passing the Sun Yat-sen Memorial Hall, you'll see the **Hall of 500 Luohan** to the right. Enter this hall through a side gate in the lower terrace of this courtyard. The gilded wood statues here (actually 508 in all) represent mythical saints (*luohan*) appointed to bear witness to Buddhist truth and save the world. You could spend years analyzing the imagery of these

Pavilion atop Incense Burner Peak

characters. Some appear to be meditating peacefully, one has a lion springing from his chest and another – an old man – tears off his skin to reveal the face of a young man.

Walk down the hill from Biyunsi the way you came but turn right into Fragrant Hills Park proper just before you reach the exit. Another translation for Xiangshan is **Incense Burner Peak**, because that's what its highest mountain (557m/1,827ft) looks like when fog rests on its summit. About 50m (55yds) along the path on the right is the ticket office for the cable car (a chair lift, actually) to the summit. This 15-minute ride (open daily 9am–4pm) gives you an all-embracing view of the park. Off to the right, you'll easily spot the Diamond Throne Pagoda. On the left are the **Spectacle Lakes (Yanjinghu)**, named for their resemblance to eye-glasses and beyond is the white glow of the luxurious Fragrant Hills Hotel.

After taking in the view from the pavilion at the top, you have two choices. To save your walking legs, hop on a cable car back to the bottom and make your way southward, visiting the Spectacle Lakes and the **Temple of Clarity (Zhaomiao)** on the way. Pass the east gate (but do not exit), walk several hundred metres along a leafy path that exits onto the main road leading to Fragrant Hills Hotel that you had a glimpse of earlier. Turn right and walk 150m (164yds) to the hotel's main entrance.

If you have the energy, the path down from Incense Burner Peak starts at the end of the pavilion farthest from the cable car terminus. It is a pleasant and not particularly demanding path, zig-zagging its way through lush forest. On the descent, which takes about 40 minutes, stay right whenever the road forks. About halfway

Chair-lift over Fragant Hills

down, you will pass an old hunting villa , and then two pavilions and lastly, the ruins of the **Fragrant Hills Temple (Xiang-shansi)**, now in the clutches of gnarled pines.

Just beyond the temple, the path will merge onto a road. Turn left and walk 100m (110yds) to the main gate of the

Fragrant Hills Hotel (Xiangshan Fandian). This oasis of luxury, designed by American Chinese architect I M Pei, embraces classical Chinese themes such as terraces, gates within gates and courtyards surrounded by halls, but adds modern angles and skylights. The grounds of the hotel are taken up by an elaborately crafted Chinese garden (plus swimming pool) that melts into the wooded surroundings. The hotel is a convenient lunch stop before you take a taxi to the Summer Palace, about 10km (6¼ miles) back in the direction of the city. The Western restaurant on the first floor and the Chinese restaurant on the second floor serve good food at moderate prices.

The **Summer Palace** or **Yiheyuan**, has a fairly checkered history. In 1888, Empress Cixi built this sprawling playground for herself with 30 million taels of silver intended for the military, while leaving China further open to foreign aggression. It was built on the site of an imperial garden of Emperor Qianlong, which had been completely destroyed and plundered by the British and French in 1860 during the Second Opium War. In 1900, a large portion of the palace was destroyed by European armies fighting the Boxers siege against foreigners in Beijing.

Palace employee

The palace is enormous – about 30sq km (12sq miles) – but the following route takes in the 'best of' without wearing out the soles of your shoes. Inside the main gate, pause to see the lavishly-furnished **Renshoudian – Hall of Benevolence and Longevity** – where the emperor held audiences with ministers and handled other state busi-

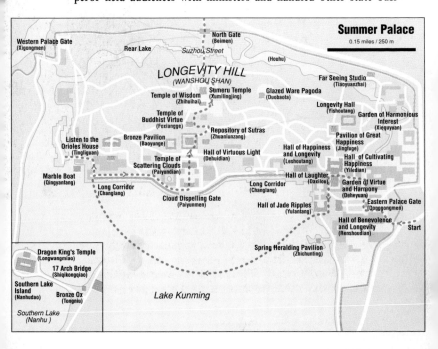

Summer Palace

0.15 miles / 250 m

Western Palace Gate (Xigongmen)

Rear Lake

North Gate (Beimen)

Suzhou Street

(Houhu)

LONGEVITY HILL (WANSHOU SHAN)

Far Seeing Studio (Tiaoyuanzhai)

Temple of Wisdom (Zhihuihai)

Sumeru Temple (Xumilingjing)

Glazed Ware Pagoda (Duobaota)

Longevity Hall (Yishoutang)

Garden of Harmonious Interest (Xiequyuan)

Temple of Buddhist Virtue (Foxiangge)

Repository of Sutras (Zhuanlunzang)

Pavilion of Great Happiness (Jingfuge)

Listen to the Orioles House (Tingliguan)

Bronze Pavilion (Baoyunge)

Hall of Virtuous Light (Dehuidian)

Hall of Happiness and Longevity (Leshoutang)

Hall of Cultivating Happiness (Yiledian)

Temple of Scattering Clouds (Paiyundian)

Marble Boat (Qingyanfang)

Long Corridor (Changlang)

Hall of Laughter (Daxilou)

Garden of Virtue and Harmony (Deheyuan)

Cloud Dispelling Gate (Paiyunmen)

Long Corridor (Changlang)

Eastern Palace Gate (Donggongmen)

Hall of Jade Ripples (Yulantang)

Hall of Benevolence and Longevity (Renshoudian)

Start

Dragon King's Temple (Longwangmiao)

17 Arch Bridge (Shiqikongqiao)

Spring Heralding Pavilion (Zhichunting)

Southern Lake Island (Nanhudao)

Bronze Ox (Tongniu)

Lake Kunming

Southern Lake (Nanhu)

A lotus-covered pond at the Summer Palace

ness during the summer months. Behind this hall, veer right to visit the **Garden of Virtue and Harmony (Deheyuan)**, the centre of which is a three-storey open-air theatre. With a system of clever trap doors between the stages, a cast of eunuchs could put up elaborate productions with immortals dropping from the sky and evil spirits rising from the depths.

Opposite the theatre is the **Hall of Laughter (Daxilou)**, where Cixi and her court sat to view the performances. It has been refurnished in the style which she was accustomed to, with her gold-coloured throne at the centre. The halls all around the periphery of the court are used for displays of court objects.

Backtrack to the **Hall of Jade Ripples (Yulantang)**, on the edge of **Lake Kunming**, where you can buy a ticket for a tour on a 'dragon boat'. The boat takes a wide sweep around the lake, so you can get a look at the **Bridge of Seventeen Arches (Shiqikongqiao)** and the **Dragon King's Temple (Longwangmiao)** on a little island in the lake. The boat docks at the far end of **Longevity Hill (Wanshou Shan)**, and if you walk another 150m (164yds) along, you can see the fanciful **Marble Boat (Qingyanfang)**. If you're not game for a steep climb over Longevity Hill, continue in this direction around the back of the hill, following the signs to Suzhou Street.

Otherwise, walk back to the boat launch area to start your amble down the **Long Corridor** or **Changlang** that runs 700m (765yds) along the northern shore of Lake Kunming. The

Long Corridor lives up to its name

entire length is intricately painted with scenes from Chinese history and legend, so be sure to stop and take in some of the lore.

Halfway along Changlang you'll come to a great triumphal arch called *pailou*, where you begin your ascent to the imposing Buddhist temple complex on the hill. The **Temple of Scattering Clouds (Paiyundian)** is where Cixi celebrated her birthdays, as evidenced by

Buddha figurines, Zhihuihai temple

the display of her birthday gifts. Beyond it is the **Hall of Virtuous Light (Dehuidian)** and then, after conquering a steep zig-zagging stone staircase, you'll have reached the octagonal **Temple of Buddhist Virtue (Foxiangge)**.

Adjacent on the west side is one of the few buildings that survived the destruction of 1860 and 1900 undamaged, the **Pavilion of Precious Clouds**. Though it looks like a wooden structure, its roof, beams, columns and struts are all cast from bronze. Climb one last stretch to the **Temple of Wisdom (Zhihuihai)**, at the top of Longevity Hill. It was built in 1750 and is covered with countless ceramic Buddha figurines. Many of the figurines within easy reach were smashed by Red Guards during the Cultural Revolution.

Just behind Zhihuihai, follow the upper path on the right side and then descend among the square towers and stupas of the **Sumeru Temple (Xumilingjing)** on your left.

At its base, you'll have your final reward in the Summer Palace, **Suzhou Street**. The thriving palace bazaar that lined the banks of a canal in Qianlong's time was beautifully restored and reopened in 1990. Little speciality shops decked with banners and lanterns are run by workers in period costumes. Browse for kites, ceramics, calligraphy and stop in a teahouse to take in its old world charm. Exit the Summer Palace on the north side of Suzhou Street.

If you have time on the way back to the city, visit the **Sakler Gallery** (officially the Arthur M Sakler Gallery of Art and Archaeology), opened on the campus of Beijing University in Spring 1993. Enter by the west gate of the university. The Sakler is the second building on the left after the bridge. It contains artifacts spanning 280,000 years, which for seven decades were stacked up in the Beijing University archaeology department. The display is well designed and not very large, so you can easily move from Paleolithic humanoids to the Qing Dynasty in a matter of 45 minutes (open daily 9am–4pm, except Monday).

Suzhou Street shopping

Ming Tombs, the Great Wall and a Shooting Range

A morning exploring the Ming tombs, followed by a picnic at the ruins. Then, a spectacular drive through the mountains and an afternoon hike on the Great Wall at Mutianyu. End the day by blasting away a few rounds on a sub-machine gun at the Beijing Great Wall Shooting Range. This is a full eight-hour day with strenuous walking.

– Ask your hotel staff to help you hire a taxi for the day. This is a 185-km (115-mile) round trip and should cost 1–2 yuan per kilometre, depending on the vehicle. Make sure the cost, duration and stop-off points are clearly understood in advance. Stress that you want to see the Great Wall at Mutianyu, not the heavily-trafficked Badaling section. There is a clearly marked, but not often taken road directly from the Ming Tombs to Mutianyu –

Ming Tombs

Of the 16 Ming Emperors who reigned from 1368 to 1644, 13 were buried about 50km (31 miles) northwest of Beijing, in a natural amphitheatre formed by mountains on three sides. Your car, moving directly north from Deshengmen Gate, traces the path the deceased royalty followed to their final resting place. About 40km (25 miles) outside the city, you'll pass through the town of Changping, which was once a garrison town partly responsible for guarding the tombs. Ironically, in Changping stands a monument to the peasant leader Li Zicheng who led the uprising that toppled the Ming Dynasty in 1644.

The **Way of the Spirit** or **Shendao** (open daily 8.30am–4.30pm), is the path over which the dead person was carried during the funeral ceremony. It begins with a white stone portico, which you'll pass a few kilometres north of Changping, and extends nearly 6½km (4 miles) to the gate of the central tomb. Five hundred metres (546yds) beyond the portico, you'll see the **Great Palace Gate**

Dragon head drain, Ding Ling

(Dagongmen) – the entrance to the royal graveyard, which covers about 15½ sq km (6sq miles). Just beyond it is the entrance to the **Avenue of the Animals**. Have the driver let you off, so you can walk through, and pick you up at the opposite end. The meaning of these 24 delightful stone creatures is still a matter of debate. Two of the creatures – the *xiezhi* and the *qilin* – are mythical animals which may have been placed for luck. Some of the familiar ones, such as elephants, camels and horses were probably meant to serve the emperor in the afterlife. Beyond the animals are 12 stone carvings of human figures – four fierce-looking soldiers, four civil officials and four scholars.

Three of the 13 tombs in this area have been officially opened as tourist sites – Ding Ling, Chang Ling and Zhao Ling. This excursion visits the first two, plus the ruins of another called De Ling. Make your first stop about 10 minutes from the Avenue of the Animals at **Ding Ling** (open daily 8am–6.30pm), burial site for the Emperor Wan Li. His is the only tomb in this area that has been excavated. Wan Li wasn't a modest fellow; this tomb cost 8 million silver taels, enough to feed a million people for 6½ years at the time. It also took 30,000 workers six years to build Ding Ling.

Ding Ling was excavated in 1956, revealing a suberannean palace of five rooms with graceful arched ceilings and filled with gold, silver, porcelain and jade treasures. To enter the vaults, pass through the courtyard, climb the **Square Tower (Fang Cheng)** and follow the paths behind. The first room you enter has a pedestal which was intended for Wan Li's concubines, but it was mysteriously empty when opened. According to one theory, this room was left empty on purpose as the court feared that repeated opening of the tomb for each successive death would allow in ill winds. The next large room contains three stone altars, which were pushed up against the massive stone slab doors leading to the room where the coffins of Wan Li and his two wives were placed along with 26 chests of treasures. Some of these items are on display at Chang Ling, your next stop. More lasting is the architectural genius invested in the graves of the Ming emperors. The massive stone slab doors, now behind glass, were designed so that another stone slab slid into place when closed, locking them from the inside.

Move on to **Chang Ling**, about a five-minute drive to the northwest. Chang Ling is the burial place for Emperor

Tomb exhibit

Yongle (1403–1424). It is the best preserved of all 13 tombs and a good example of how they were organized. In the front section, a large courtyard filled with twisted pines leads to a sacrificial hall. This one, called **Ling'en Dian** (open daily 8am–6.30pm) is supported by 32 giant pillars, each made from a tree. The yellow colour of the glazed tiles and dragon head drains are symbols reserved for the emperor. At one time, a funeral tablet lay on a wooden altar at the centre of this room and sacrifices were made in front of it. This hall now contains an exhibition of items found in Ding Ling – from jewelled hairpins to suits of armour and the rich dragon brocade used in imperial dress.

Chang Ling

The second section is a courtyard in which stands a stele tower, basically a fancy grave marker for the emperor. Just behind is the burial mound, or tumulus, enclosed by a wall about 500m (546yds) long. Presumably, it contains Yongle's coffin and other burial treasures. To the east and west are burial grounds for his 16 concubines who, by some accounts, were buried alive to bring pleasure to the emperor in the next world.

Last stop at the tombs takes you to De Ling. This is where you part ways with the vendors, so you may want to pick up, some drinks before leaving Chang Ling. **De Ling**, about 10 minutes drive southwest, is where Wan Li's grandson, Emperor Xi Zong (1621–1627) is buried. Known for being an enthusiastic carpenter and an inattentive ruler, Xi Zong lost power to his eunuchs. It seems somehow appropriate that his tomb is seedy and weedy, with ceremonial urns strewn about as if there had been a brawl. Find a perch for your picnic, but don't smoke here, lest you suffer the wrath of the villager who looks after it.

Backtrack to Chang Ling, In the far corner of the parking lot, about 100m (110yds) from the entrance, you'll see a sign which says in Chinese '**Great Wall at Mutianyu**' and then, more comprehensible to the non-Chinese speaker, '37km'. This is a beautiful drive on a two-lane road that winds its way eastward through villages and mountains. It's a bit further than the Badaling section but well worth the trek. The only confusing point is a fork in the road just 400m (436yds) from the start. Take the left branch.

Great Wall guardian

No question about the wall, it's big. Adding together all the sections, it extends, in various states of repair, more than 3,862km (2,400 miles), twisting and doubling back from the coast all the way to the central province of Gansu. Chinese propaganda asserts

that this is the only man-made structure that can be seen from the moon, but now it is rumoured to share that honour with the Staten Island garbage dump. At any rate, it's a terrific look-out point for a soldier, or a tourist.

The path up to the wall takes a good 20 minutes. You can save your energy for the wall itself by taking the cable car.

The Great Wall, which is called 'Ten Thousand Mile Wall' in Chinese, originated as a labyrinth of small walls, built around warring king-doms in the north as early as the 5th century BC. The first Qin emperor, Shi Huangdi, having united China for the first time in 221BC, became obsessed with the idea of linking sections to create a vast barrier from the barbarians in the north. Like the pyramids, the wall has its dark side. Countless thousands of poor peasants were conscripted to build it, and many died doing so.

As the Mongol invasion showed, your wall is only as strong as those who guard it. Even so, after the Ming threw the Mongols out, the wall project was resumed with a vengeance. Mutianyu dates to the Ming period (1368–1644), as does most of what remains of the wall. It was restored and opened to tourists in 1986. If you are ambitious and climb to the end of the restored section, you'll see the wall in its natural state of decay.

The road returning to Beijing is about 75km (46½ miles) due south, entering the city at Dongzhimen. If you have time and ag-gression to work out, stop on the way back at the **Beijing Great Wall Shooting Range** (open daily 8am–6.30pm), 14km (9 miles) south of Mutianyu on a little road leading east. Try your hand at skeets, laser shooting or a truly cathartic round on a sub-ma-chine gun. This is one of thou-sands of money-making ven-tures run by the Chinese military, who after all, are not about to be left out of the re-form-era boom.

Stallone wanna-be

Morning Itineraries

1. Temple of Heaven, Natural History Museum and Hongqiao Farmers' Market

Early morning rituals at the Temple of Heaven Park, followed by an exploration of the grounds; a stop at the Natural History Museum and shopping at the Hongqiao Farmers' Market.

– Take a taxi or trolley bus No 106 to the north gate of the Temple of Heaven Park –

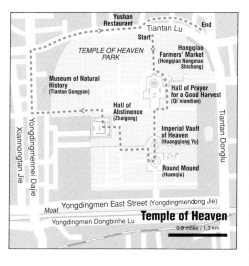

Temple of Heaven

Temple of Heaven (**Tiantan**) refers to the park (open daily 6am–8pm) enclosed by a wall 5km (3 miles) long. Getting there by 7am will allow you to catch a glimpse of the action: practitioners of Chinese *qigong* regulating and strengthening their internal systems through concentration and breathing exercises. Elsewhere, you will see slow-motion martial arts – *taiqi* and sword dancing, disco dancing, and a recent addition, aerobics classes!

The Temple of Heaven complex was first built between 1406 and 1420 under Emperor Yongle as a sacred place where the emperor, the designated Son of Heaven, could appeal to Heaven on behalf of his kingdom. The park is round in the north, representing Heaven, and square in the south, representing the Earth. Sacred symbols pervade even minute details of its design. Each year, just before the

Listening to the Whispering Wall

winter solstice, the emperor and his retinue of cavalrymen and eunuchs would begin a procession from the Forbidden City, through Qianmen, to the Temple of Heaven. After fasting and meditating, the emperor would have a one-on-one with Heaven, the only authority he recognized. This ritual, which lasted until 1914, goes back as far as 4,000 years, centuries before Buddhism and other religions delivered their pantheon of deities to the court.

Find your way to the city's most elegant and possibly most well-recognized structure – the **Hall of Prayer for a Good Harvest (Qi'niandian)**. The blue-glazed tile roof representing heaven is supported by four 18-m (60-ft) high pillars, one for each of the four seasons. The other 24 pillars standing in two concentric circles symbolize the months of the year and the hours of the day. Intricate framework creates the dome high overhead; below are thrones where tablets commemorating the ancestors were placed. Interestingly, not a single nail was used in constructing this building. The original hall was burned down and was faithfully rebuilt in 1889.

Head south to the **Imperial Vault of Heaven**, much smaller but with a similarly striking blue-tile roof. The ancestor tablets were stored here until needed in the prayer ceremony. It is now best

The distinctive Hall of Prayer for a Good Harvest

known for its acoustical magic. Stand on the first **Echo Stone** in front of the entrance to the hall and clap; you will hear a single echo. Do the same on the second stone and you will hear a double echo, and on the third, a triple. The **Whispering Wall**, which embraces the courtyard around the hall, transmits a normal speaking voice to its opposite side. Walk south to the **Round Mound** where three concentric terraces stand inside two enclosures – one square and one round. Animal sacrifices were burnt in furnaces inside the square enclosure while the emperor prayed at the centre of the mound.

On the way to the west exit of the temple, you'll pass through the courtyard of the **Hall of Abstinence (Zhaigong)**. This is where the emperor fasted and meditated in the hours preceding the dawn of the solstice. The hall has a double moat spanned by a series of fine stone bridges, and its courtyard has a lovely drum and bell tower.

Exit by the west gate, just north of the Hall of Abstinence. Outside the gate, you'll run into the main North–South street, Tianqiao Nandajie, after walking about 100m (109yds). Turn right and walk about 300m (327yds) to the **Museum of Natural History**, filled with all sorts of creepy crawly things on display, including the Yangtze River sturgeon, which grows to more than 5m (5½yds) in length, and the freshwater Yangtze alligator, a species found only in China.

Grab a taxi for a five-minute ride to the northeast corner of the park to **Hongqiao Farmers' Market** (open daily 7am–5.30pm). This covered market curving along Tiantan Road has it all: furniture, leather products, freshwater pearls, antiques, curios and spices.

Hongqiao Farmers' Market

For lunch, backtrack about 400m (436yds) to the north gate of the Temple of Heaven. Across Tiantan Road, and slightly to the left, you'll see **Yushan Restaurant** (No 87 Tiantan Lu, Tel: 701-4263. Open daily 10.30am–1.30pm, 4.30–7.30pm) which specializes in Manchu-Han imperial banquets. Try the sesame cake with minced pork filling – the Chinese answer to the hamburger.

2. Marco Polo Bridge, Ox Street Mosque and Fayuansi Buddhist Temple

The highlights of southwest Beijing, beginning with the Marco Polo Bridge in the suburb of Wanping and then visiting two working religious centres.

– Take a mini-van or taxi to Wanping, 15km (9 miles) south of Beijing. Have the driver wait or you may be forced to make a gruelling trip back by bus No 339 –

In the 13th century, Marco Polo was on his way back to the West as an emissary of Kublai Khan when he encountered **Lugouqiao**, a stone bridge spanning the Yongding River. He gave it such rave reviews that Europeans dubbed it the **Marco Polo Bridge**. The bridge was built in 1189 during the Jin Dynasty and rebuilt in the same style in 1698 after being badly damaged by a flood. It is an impressive structure, with 140 columns, each topped with stone carvings of lions. Today, only pedestrians and bicycles are allowed, but until a few years ago all traffic traversed it. At one end of the

Marco Polo Bridge

bridge is a small exhibition room (open daily 9am–5pm, except Monday) explaining the bridge's and the town's history.

In Polo's day, **Wanping** was a busy little riverside town full of inns and restaurants where merchants stopped to load up with goods. Under a grand scheme announced several years ago by top government leaders, the old town was to be recreated, with some extras like a horse track, paddle boats and Qing-style homes. The city wall was rebuilt and the gate towers restored, but there was insufficient money for the other plans. There were also logistical problems: since a reservoir was built upstream, there has been no water under the bridge. From the traveller's point of view though, this is probably a blessing; Wanping is typical of sleepy, rural China.

Wanping's second claim to fame is the July 7 Incident of 1937, when a clash between Chinese and Japanese soldiers triggered off Japan's invasion into China at the start of World War II. In the centre of Wanping, about 10 minutes' walk into town along the main street, is the **Memorial Hall of the War of Resistance Against Japan** (open daily 9am–5pm, except Monday). This glowing marble edifice contains an interesting pictorial account of World War II from a Chinese perspective.

Have your driver drop you at **Ox Street Mosque** (open daily 4am–8pm). Built in AD996 in purely Arabic style, this is the oldest and largest of about 50 mosques in Beijing. Islam was introduced to China during the Tang Dynasty (AD618–907) by Arab merchants. The central tower of the mosque is the 'moon-watching tower' for the *Imam* (priest) to fix the precise time of the start and end of fast during *Ramadan* or fasting month. Prayer takes place five times a day in the main prayer hall, which faces Mecca (west). Over the centuries though, the original architecture has been replaced by Chinese details, including the familiar line of little animals guarding the eaves. But inside the hall and towers, there are no graven images – animal or human – as this is prohibited by the Koran. Instead, geometric designs and Arabic lettering adorn the walls.

Ox Street Mosque is an active place of worship and gathering point for Beijing's Mus-

Ox Street Mosque

lim community which numbers about 180,000. Female visitors need not cover their heads when entering the mosque but non-Muslim visitors cannot enter the prayer hall.

To get to Fayuansi Buddhist Temple, take a 15- to 20-minute walk through the *hutongs* (alleys). Turn right on Ox Street (Niujie) as you leave the mosque. About 100m (109yds) along, turn right again onto Shuru Hutong which has a Chinese archway at its entrance. It's easy to spot where the wealthy lived: entrances to better courtyard homes are marked with more elaborate *mendui* – two carved stones placed on either side of the door. Walk along Shuru Hutong for about 500m (545yds). About midway, cross one wide *hutong* identifiable by a public toilet in the corner. At the end of Shuru, turn right onto Xizhuan Hutong. Walk about 400m (436yds) and take a right into Fayuansi Qianhutong. The temple gate is just 50m (55yds) after the turn.

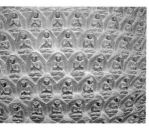
Bronze statuary, Fayuansi

Fayuansi, the **Temple of the Source of the Law** (open daily 8.30–11am, 1–4pm), is one of the oldest and most pleasant Buddhist temples in Beijing. It was built in AD645 and called *Minzhongsi* (Temple in Memory of the Loyal) to commemorate soldiers who died in battle. Today, it is a quiet monastery with about 40 monks. Many of the figures within are fine bronzes, some dating to the Ming Dynasty. In the final hall at the rear is a 6-m (19½-ft) long sleeping Buddha.

From here, take a cab to your next destination. If you're hungry, turn right onto Niujie and walk about 600m (654yds) to **Tonghexuan**, a homely little restaurant serving Muslim food on the left. Try the *shuanyangrou* – mutton and vegetables boiled together in a pot at your table.

3. Beijing Hotel and the Foreign Legation Quarter

Breakfast at the Beijing Hotel and an architectural tour of early 20th-century Beijing through the former Foreign Legation Quarter.

– Take bus Nos 2, 10 or 20, or trolley bus Nos 101, 103 or 109 to Tiananmen Square and walk east one block to Beijing Hotel on Chang'an Avenue. This itinerary is a moderate 2–2½ hour walk, but you can also bike. Bicycles for rent at the bike park on the east end of the Beijing Hotel –

The gargantuan **Beijing Hotel** was built during four different eras and the mood of the day is reflected in the hotel's different wings. Start at the east end. Bleak, square and utilitarian, this section was built in 1974 as the Cultural Revolution was burning out and just two years before Mao's death. Next is the oldest existing section. Built in 1917, the ornate French-style vaulted ceilings, arched windows and stairway sweeping up through the centre evoke images of the decadent 1920s. The French-style cafe in this section (open daily 7am–9pm) is a nice and quiet spot for morning coffee. Beyond is the extension built in 1954, during the optimism that followed the Communist victory. Its bracketed ceiling and lanterns are Chinese-style and there is a lavish banquet room where foreign government officials were once entertained. The westernmost section, the Grand Hotel, is an eclectic 1989 addition and a tribute to the new money of the reform era.

French-style cafe

The turn-of-the-century European architecture in China is a reminder of the ignominious decline of the Qing Dynasty and the foreign domination that followed. The **Foreign Legation Quarter**, south of the Beijing Hotel and east of Tiananmen Square, contains some elegant European buildings which recall part of modern China's history. Between the 1860s and the outbreak of the Sino-Japanese war in 1937, 13 foreign governments were represented here, their presence forced on the Chinese by the outcome of the Opium Wars. They had their own administration, police, churches, hospitals, shops and post office, guarded by some 1,000 soldiers. After 1900, when the Boxers launched a 45-day attack here, it was completely closed off to Chinese nationals.

Exit Beijing Hotel at its east end. At the traffic light where Taijichang Street (Customs Street) intersects Chang'an Avenue, cross the latter and follow Taijichang southwards. About 200m (218yds) along on the right, you'll come to the gate of the former **Italian Legation**, where the Italians moved in 1900 after the Boxers de-

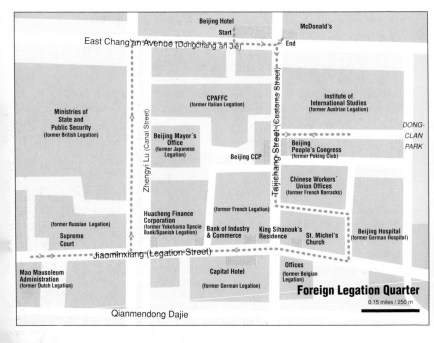

Beijing Hotel
Start
McDonald's
East Chang'an Avenue (Dongchang an Jie) — End

Ministries of State and Public Security (former British Legation)

CPAFFC (former Italian Legation)

Institute of International Studies (former Austrian Legation)

DONG-CLAN PARK

Zhengyi Lu (Canal Street)

Beijing Mayor's Office (former Japanese Legation)

Beijing CCP

Taijichang Street (Customs Street)

Beijing People's Congress (former Peking Club)

Chinese Workers' Union Offices (former French Barracks)

(former Russian Legation)
Supreme Court

Huacheng Finance Corporation (former Yokohama Specie Bank/Spanish Legation)

(former French Legation)

Bank of Industry & Commerce

King Sihanouk's Residence

St. Michel's Church

Beijing Hospital (former German Hospital)

Jiaominxiang (Legation Street)

Mao Mausoleum Administration (former Dutch Legation)

Capital Hotel
(former German Legation)

Offices (former Belgian Legation)

Foreign Legation Quarter

0.15 miles / 250 m

Qianmendong Dajie

stroyed their previous quarters. It now houses the **Chinese People's Association for Friendship with Foreign Countries** (CPAFFC).

Continue along Taijichang Street but cross to the opposite side. Walk alongside a high gray wall topped with curved tiles and turn left into the first alleyway. About 200m (218yds) on the left is the gate to the former **Austrian Legation**, now the **Institute of International Studies**. Built in 1900, the simple grey and white building has changed hands many times. In 1915, when China declared war on Germany and its allies, the building was occupied by the Hungarians. After a short spell under the Dutch, a Russian general turned it into a guesthouse in the late 1920s. In 1938, it became the German Club. The Americans used it for Allied Property Administration and the Hungarians for an embassy later. The building was finally returned to the Chinese in 1969.

Double back to Taijichang Street and turn left. Through the first gate on the left is an elegant grey-blue building with arches along the ground floor, topped by a red national emblem and a single portal. This is the headquarters of the **Beijing People's Congress** (no entry to the public). Built in 1902, this was once the **Peking Club** – with a swimming pool and tennis courts that were still used as late as the 1960s. The white building directly opposite, topped with an enormous red star, is the headquarters for the Beijing municipality **Communist Party Committee** (CCP).

Moving on along Taijichang, you'll enter 'Little France'. The French, along with the British, were the first to install permanent diplomatic representatives here and they held large tracts of land on both sides of the street. On the right side of the street are the graceful roof lines of the former French Legation. Turn left on the second alleyway, about 200m (218yds) beyond the Peking Club. French theologian Teilhard de Chardin, who lived in China from 1932 to 1946, founded an institute of geobiology on this street. Much of this area has been replaced with typical Chinese apartment blocks but about 100m (109yds) along on the left, you can peer through the French Barracks's gates. The Soviet-style building at the centre is the **Chinese Workers' Union** offices.

Continue another 100m (109yds) along this alleyway and turn right. After another 100m (109yds), you'll reach Jiaominxiang Street (Legation Street). Turn right again. Just before the next intersection, about 200m (218yds) along on the right is **St Michel's Church,** an intimate little neo-Gothic-style church built by the French Vincentian Order in 1902. St Michel's was closed after the 1949 revolution, but was renovated and reopened in 1989. During the week, you can enter the chapel from a door on the right side, but keep quiet as there are usually people

St Michel's Church

worshipping. The figures of the saints above the doors date to 1889 and some of the stained glass and ceramic tiles are original.

Opposite the church, you can see jagged brick roof lines and green tops of the former **Belgian Legation**. Before 1900, this was the home of a high level Chinese official, Xu Tong, who hated foreigners so much he said he wished to cover his sedan chair with their skin. He did his best to avoid the barbarians, and when the Allied armies entered Beijing in 1900 in reaction to the Boxer Rebellion, Xu Tong could take it no longer. He committed suicide.

From St Michel's, cross Taijichang Street and continue along Jiaominxiang Street. About 50m (55yds) past the intersection,

Former French Legation

where two massive stone lions and two armed soldiers stand guard, are the red gates of the former **French Legation**. This is now the occasional residence of Cambodian King Norodom Sihanouk, a favour from the Chinese government when he went into exile. Across the road is the gate for the former offices of Jardine Matheson, one of the earliest and most aggressive Western trading companies in Asia.

About 200m (218yds) further along Jiaominxiang Street, you'll pass a tiny building on the right with fancy brickwork, a zig-zag roof line and arched windows. This is now a branch of the **Bank of Industry and Commerce**, but until recently, it was a post office. This was also the site of the original Beijing Hotel before it moved to its current location in 1900. Next to it is the beginning of the former **Spanish Legation** (which used to extend all the way to the corner) where the protocol on the Boxer Rebellion was signed in 1901. The Spanish sold the corner lot to the Yokohama Specie Bank, now the **Huacheng Finance Corporation**. Empress Dowager Cixi was said to have borrowed money here just before the last dynasty fell. The valuables she put up as collateral were never reclaimed and are now in a collection in London.

The Huacheng Finance Corporation stands on the corner of Jiaominxiang and Zhengyi roads, the divided north-south street. 'Zhengyi' means 'jus-

Huacheng Finance Corporation

tice', but the road used to be called Canal Street because there was a trench that carried sewage water. It was filled in 1925 to create the promenade between the two lanes.

Cross Zhengyi Road and continue on Jiaominxiang. On the right side behind the row of fruit vendors is where once stood the Russian Orthodox Mission, which later became the **Russian Legation** and then the Soviet Legation. Until 1991, there was a simple stone building here – probably the former Russian church. Now there is a shiny white building housing the **Supreme Court**. Three hundred metres (327yds) further down is a block-like, brown brick structure with a green roof on the left side. This is the former **Dutch Legation**. It now houses the **Mao Mausoleum Administration**. Across the street are vendors selling steaming bowls of hand-pulled noodles. If you're due for a break, this is a pleasant snack.

Retrace your steps along Jiaominxiang Street and turn left on Zhengyi Road for the final stretch. The area on the right side of Zhengyi Road, north of the Huacheng Finance Corporation, was the **Japanese Legation**. It now houses the **Beijing mayor's office** and the offices of the city government.

The last, and possibly grandest relic of this walk is a bit farther along Zhengyi Road on the left: the former **British Legation**. The British moved in after the Opium War of 1860 and expanded the area to become the largest territory held by foreigners. They kept this compound until 1959, but it is now occupied by the **Ministries of State and Public Security**, the Chinese version of the KGB. Note the elegant sweeping roof lines now adorned with satellite dishes.

The Legation loop brings you to the corner of Zhengyi Road and Chang'an Avenue, across the Beijing Hotel. Take the western colonial theme to its logical conclusion and eat at the world's largest **McDonald's** which seats 701 people. To get there, turn right on Chang'an Avenue, walk to the next corner and cross Chang'an.

Afternoon Itineraries

4. Lama Temple, Confucius Temple and Ditan Park

An introduction to two different Chinese philosophical traditions, topped off with dinner and dancing at Ditan Park. The three sites are situated within a 1km (½ mile) radius so the tour is an easy walk or bike ride.

– Take the subway to Yonghegong station (which stops under the temple). After leaving the station, turn left onto Yonghegong Dongsi Beidajie. The main gate of Lama Temple (Yonghegong) is 75m (82yds) away on the left –

Buddhism came to China from India as early as the 1st century, but Lamaism – the highly mystical sect of Tibetan Buddhism represented by the Lama Temple – made inroads after the Mongols conquered Tibet in the 13th century. During the Qing Dynasty, several emperors were proponents of this sect, as much to appease the Buddhist fringes of the kingdom as for religious reasons. The temple was formerly home to Emperor Yongzheng before he ascended the throne. His son, Emperor Qianlong, converted it into a Lamaist monastery in 1744 and it remained so until 1960.

Lama Temple, **Yonghegong** (open daily 9am–4.30pm, closed Monday) is a typical Tibetan monastery. It consists of five halls and three gates laid out along an axis. In each hall, the central Buddhist figure is more imposing than the last; the one in the fifth hall stands three-storeys high. The most elegant is the fourth. Today, there are about 70 monks from the ages of 17 to 80 living at the Lama Temple. A word of advice: many of the monks are clearly irritated at being photographed. Find out if its okay before you point and shoot. No photos are allowed inside the halls.

Tibetan Buddhism is a benign and introspective religion today, but it hasn't always been so. Human sacrifice used to be part of its rituals. Take a close look at the carvings and Tibetan *thangka* paintings in the halls along the side. One memorable image is of the goddess Lamo riding a horse cloaked in the skin of her own son, whom, the story goes, she had sacrificed to show her detachment from the world.

In the communist era, relations between the authorities and top Buddhist leaders have been rocky. The current Dalai Lama – the spiritual leader believed to be an incarnation of the Buddha – fled to India in 1959 after failing to win independence for Tibet. Though the government is still officially atheist, during the re-

Lama Temple roof detail

form years churches and temples, including the Lama Temple, have been being restored, along with the right to worship. The Dalai Lama is still condemned by Beijing but his image, once forbidden, can now be displayed in temple exhibits.

Next stop is the **Confucius Temple (Kong Miao)**. Go west on Guozijian Jie, the street that runs into Yonghegong Street about 20 paces north of the main gate to the temple. The entrance to the Confucius Temple (open daily 9am–4.30pm) is about 200m (218yds) along, on the north side.

Confucius was a teacher in the state of Lu (present day Shandong Province) in the 6th century BC, about the same time as Buddha was teaching in India. Unlike Buddhism, Confucianism focused on order, not spiritual enlightenment. It teaches that if a ruler is moral and follows the proper rites and rituals for his station in life, his subjects will fall in line. The same is true for husbands and wives, parents and children.

In the first of the four courtyards of this 14th-century temple is a series of 188 stone tablets resembling tombstones. The tablets bear the names of scholars who passed imperial examinations here. The halls have high ornate ceilings but are left comparatively unadorned.

Main Hall, Confucius Temple

By this time, you'll be ready for some earthly pleasures – food, song and dance. Proceed to **Ditan Park** or **Altar of the Earth** (open daily 6am–9pm) by returning to Yonghegong Street and walking north. The entrance to the park is just 300m (327yds) north of the Yonghegong subway station, on the left side.

Ditan Park, first built in 1530, had a similar ritual function to the Temple of Heaven. Each year on the Summer solstice throughout the Ming and Qing dynasties, the emperor came here to make animal sacrifices and pray. These grounds were off-limits to ordinary mortals until after 1911. The mound, a round platform surrounded by two concentric square walls where the sacrifice was offered, was restored in the 1980s.

To the west of the mound area, a hall that once housed the sacred tablets, and later held weapons, has been restored and converted into the **Fangzitan Arts and Crafts Store** (open daily 9.30am–8pm). Around the mound to the north side is **Fengrusong Restaurant** (open daily 7.30am–9pm) which serves good Cantonese dishes. The menu is in Chinese, but the waitresses speak some English. Ask for the prices of dishes when you order as they range from 15 yuan to 350 yuan! After dinner, grab your partner and

Fengrusong Restaurant

join in one of the truly civilized pastimes of modern China – ballroom dancing. A 'dance party' is held nightly (7.30–9.30pm, if weather permits, from March–mid-October) at **Li Yue Yuan Flower Garden**, about 200m (218yds) north of Fengrusong Restaurant. Just follow the 'oom-pah-pah' of the live band. Ditan's entrepreneurs have also just opened a karaoke bar in the Zaishengting – a hall once used to prepare sacrificial animals. The **Hancheng Karaoke Bar** (open daily 8pm–2am) is southwest of the shopping area. The park officially closes at 9pm, but the gate is open all night to accommodate ballroom dancers and karaoke customers.

5. Old Outer City Districts – Dashalar and Liulichang

A walk through the hutongs of two neighbourhoods outside Zhengyangmen (Qianmen) Gate. Takes between 30 minutes and three hours depending on whether you stop to shop.

– Take the subway to Qianmen Station and cross to the corner southwest from Tiananmen Square (by the Kentucky Fried Chicken and Vie de France) –

Dashalar, extending south and west from Zhengyangmen (Qianmen) gate, was once synonymous with decadence, squalor and overindulgence of every kind. During the Ming and Qing dynasties, the district was full of theatres, teahouses, brothels and beggars. All the vulgar activities forbidden in the Imperial City flourished here for off-duty merchants and bureaucrats. Even a bored prince would occasionally appear incognito for a naughty night out.

If you're facing the Vie de France, turn left and then veer right, following the street as it rounds the traffic circle just south of Tiananmen Square. Walk about 100m (109yds) between two rows of densely-packed food and clothing vendors. Turn right onto **Zhubaoshi Jie (Jewellery Street)**, in the heart of the market. Zhubaoshi Jie runs parallel to Qianmen Street, its entrance marked by an enormous Phoenix Bicycle billboard.

1 Neiliansheng Shoe Store
2 Tong Ren Traditional Medicine Shop
3 Zhang Yiyuan Tea Shop
4 Underground City
5 Ruifuxiang Fabric Store
6 Qianmen Women's Clothing Store

Xuanwumen Street
Qianmen East Street
Kentucky Fried Chicken
Vie de France
Tiananmen Square
Dongdajie
Start
Qianmen (Zhengyangmen) Gate
Nanxinghua
Confucian Tradition Restaurant
Rongbaozhai
Jewellery
Qianmen
5 6
End
Liulichang Jie
Liulichang District
Liulichang East Street
Yangmei Alley
Street (Zhubaoshi Jie)
Street
Street
1 2 3 4
Dashalar
Dashalar and Liulichang
0.3 miles / 500 m
Dashalar District

There are bargains galore here, although some of the products are of dubious quality. With hawkers shouting prices from all sides, music blaring, and egg vendors and pedicabs pushing their way through the crowd, it's easy to imagine Dashalar at the turn of the century. What you aren't likely to find today are the painted ladies that once populated this district. Once a deeply entrenched feature of Dashalar, prostitution all but disappeared under the Communists. There were various classes of brothels and during the Republican period; the women were even registered with the government and given regular health check-ups.

About 300m (327yds) along, Zhubaoshi Jie intersects with **Dashalar Street**, a wide and bustling alley with a green-coloured police security booth on the left side of the corner. Turn right at this point. About 20m (22yds) along on the right is a building with extravagant wrought iron gratework in green. This is the **Qianmen Women's Clothing Store** (open daily 8.30am–9pm). If you're thinking of having clothes tailored in China, you may want to check out the wide selection of wool and other suit materials on the second floor.

Dashalar bazaar

The same goes for the **Ruifuxiang Silk and Cotton Fabric Store** (open daily 8.30am–9.30pm) two doors down, with a pretentious marble entryway. Ruifuxiang was built here in 1893 by a Shandong businessman and catered to society's upper crust, including Yuan Shikai – a shortlived president who rose to power after the fall of the Qing dynasty – as well as wives and concubines of the Imperial Court.

At No 18 Dashalar Street, return for a moment to the Socialist era with a visit to the **Underground City** (open daily 8am–5pm). Its entrance is marked by a sign in English that reads 'Underground City' and has an arrow pointing down a flight of stairs in a clothing store to the left. In the late 1960s, during China's Cold War with the Soviet Union, Mao Zedong ordered the construction of a huge system of air raid shelters, which still remains in cities throughout China. The whole Beijing tunnel system is reportedly 3km (1¾ miles) long. The part that you can see in Dashalar is 270m (295yds) long, in some places as deep as 15m (49ft) below ground. It was hand-built by 2,000 volunteers under army supervision. No 18 is one of 90 entrances to this section. Today, it is a

Tongren Pharmacy

dank-smelling arcade with a 100-bed hotel that was originally a hospital.

Back on the surface and still on the left side, just a few doors beyond the Underground City at No 22 is **Zhang Yiyuan Tea Shop** (open daily 8am–7.30pm) with bas-relief flower designs under its windows. This is a good place for your favourite tea. Just next door at No 24 is the **Tongren Traditional Chinese Medicine Shop** (open daily 8am–9.30pm), once responsible for keeping secret medicinal recipes for the emperor. It's been around since 1669 and the pharmacist still weighs age-old herbal prescriptions with a hand-held scale. Look out for the incredible array of cures from deer antlers to ginseng for curing impotence and enhancing the libido.

Further down is an ornate and traditional Chinese-style four-storey building, the **Neiliansheng Shoe Store**, built in 1853. There is nothing traditional about the interior of Neiliansheng though. It's been redone in chrome and glass and features Chinese-made platform shoes, trainers and stiletto heels. You can be shod cheaply and in style here, but only if your feet are fairly delicate – American size 8½ or smaller.

After walking about 300m (327yds) on Dashalar, you'll arrive at another intersection with a little green police security booth. Turn right and then another 30m (33yds) later, left. This is **Yangmei Alley**, an average Beijing *hutong* with children, old people and the smells of cooking and communal toilets all merged together. Most of the doors lead into *siheyuan*, courtyards with rooms on all sides facing the centre. Life in these homes is not particularly comfortable. In summer, the heat drives the inhabitants out to the streets. In winter, most homes are heated by coal-burning stoves.

After another 400m (436yds) or so, Yangmei Alley takes a little jog to the right where you'll see an antique shop on your left. Turn left to **Liulichang**, a charmingly restored section of the old city jam-packed with curios, carpets and antiques. This has been a market-place for books and antiques for more than 300 years. During the Ming dynasty, Liulichang, which means 'glazed-tile factory', was one of the sites where tiles were made for the imperial buildings. Later, it was developed into a cultural centre for scholar-officials who stocked up on calligraphy supplies, books and seals. Check out

Liulichang street scene

Rongbaozhai (open daily 9am–6pm), a 17th-century shop at No 19, famous for its watercolour block paintings, rubbings and reproductions of old paintings.

For dinner, head for the **Confucian Heritage Restaurant** (open daily 10.30am–1.30pm; 4.30–8pm), a cozy little teahouse at No 3 that specializes in saucy Shandong dishes with curious names. What is Supernatural Duck anyway?

6. The Lake District

Explore the ancient Drum and Bell Towers and a farmers' market; walk along the lakes and dine in the imperial gardens of Beihai Park. Walk, or bike if you prefer.

– Take a taxi to the Drum and Bell Towers. You'll spot the towers just north of the intersection of Di'anmen Dajie and Gulou Dongdajie. Or you could take public bus No 204 or trolley bus No 107, both of which stop just 50m (55yds) from the Drum Tower –

Browse around the lively market in the old neighbourhood between the Drum Tower and the Bell Tower. Here, you'll find live shrimp, spices sold in bulk, vegetables and home-made noodles. The covered market at the centre is a good place to become acquainted with Beijing's snack foods. Try *shaobing* (griddle fried cakes with sesame seeds on top), *baodu* (sheep stomach strips), *qiehe* (deep-fried eggplant), *chao tianluo* (fried river snails) and *douzhi* (a milky substance made from beans). Stick to hot-off-the-stove cooked food; this market is very earthy.

The grey **Bell Tower (Zhonglou)** and the red **Drum Tower (Gulou)** are the legacy of Kublai Khan who had the first ones built nearby to serve as the city clock. The drums were sounded to signal the closing of the city gates and the changing of night sentries while the bell struck the time of day. As with most Mongol buildings, the two towers were replaced in 1420, during the Ming dynasty. The Drum Tower is a 15th-century structure. The Bell Tower, which was made of wood, burned down and was later rebuilt of stone in 1747.

Both towers (open daily 9am–4.30pm) are open to visitors. The Bell Tower is more interesting inside. Its stone staircase leads through a cool stone passageway that brings to mind medieval castles. In 1990, the bell was re-installed in the tower and since then

Bell Tower

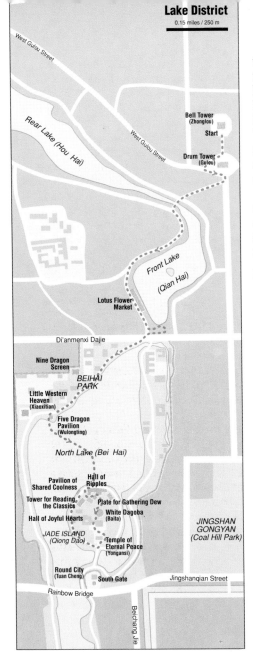

Lake District

0.15 miles / 250 m

the mayor has climbed the tower at every Spring Festival to ring in the Lunar New Year. In the hall atop the Drum Tower, the tattered remains of one of the 24 original drums are on display.

To start your walk around the lakes, go south on Di'anmen Dajie and turn right on the first alleyway you meet, about 50m (55yds) along. This narrow lane leads past a line of hairdressers and old guesthouses. Another 150m (164yds) along is an intersection. Turn left at this point. Ahead is a little stone bridge that divides **Houhai (Rear Lake)** from **Qianhai (Front Lake)**. The two are part of a string of six lakes extending all the way from the north to the south of the old Inner City.

Cross the little stone bridge and turn left on the path that runs along the shore of Qianhai. The south end of Qianhai is where the action is. About 700m (765yds) along on the southwest shore is the **Lotus Flower Market**, a great place to hang around until late at night and savour Beijing snacks. Round the southwest corner of the lake is a large shady area. When the weather is fine, musicians gather under the trees with their traditional instruments and create a marvellous cacophony. The lake draws swimmers in the summer, skaters in the winter and strollers all year round.

Cross Di'anmen Xidajie – the main street passing Qianhai on the south – and just off to the right is the north entrance to **Beihai**

(North Lake) Park (open daily 6am–10pm). The area around this lake and south of it has served as imperial residence or gardens for every dynasty that had its capital in Beijing. Beihai was opened to the public in 1925, after the end of the imperial era, but Nanhai (South Lake) and Zhonghai (Central Lake) have remained the cloistered domain of the Chinese leadership – Zhongnanhai.

The focal point of the park is **Jade Island (Qiong Dao)** with its white dagoba resembling a dollop of whipped cream. But first skirt the western shore to see the **Nine Dragon Screen**, one of three in the city. It's just past the gate with three arches. Emperor Qianlong had the screen built to protect the temple behind it from fire. Unfortunately, the temple burned down and now there is a sports complex behind it. Scholars say the screen has 635 dragons, including those in the eaves.

Next stop is **Xiaoxitian**, 200m (218yds) along the shore line from the Nine Dragon Screen. **Little Western Heaven**, as it is aptly named, was built in 1770 as a shrine to the Goddess of Mercy, Guanyin – a large square pagoda surrounded by a moat and four guard towers. Backtrack to the **Five Dragon Pavilion (Wulongting)**, named after the zig-zagging walkways that link them, as if the mythical beast was snaking along the shore.

Just north of the Five Dragon Pavilion, board a ferry to Jade Island (every half hour, 9am–6pm). The boat stops in front of the Fangshan Restaurant, your dinner destination, but first explore the imperial gardens while there's still light.

The restaurant is located in a complex called the **Hall of Ripples**, (the names only become more poetic from here). Go right on the covered walkway – the **Pavilion of Shared Coolness** – and take the stone path leading up the hill just beyond. Climb the hill to the **Plate for Gathering Dew**, which is a cast bronze figure of a man holding a container over his head. Emperor Qianlong built this whimsical tribute to a Han Dynasty emperor who ordered his assistants to collect dew, which he believed was an elixir for immortality. Along the northwest side of the hill is the **Tower for Reading the Classics**, containing a set of stone tablets with calligraphy dating back to the 6th or 7th century.

At the summit of Jade Island glows the **White Dagoba (Baita)**, built by the first Qing emperor in 1651 to mark the Dalai Lama's first visit to Beijing. After it was damaged in the Tangshan earthquake of 1976, workmen doing restoration work discovered a repository in its base containing a host of religious objects, including two bone fragments which were very likely relics from eminent lamas.

White Dagoba in the distance

Descend the south side of the hill and pass through the **Hall for Joyful Hearts** – an official meeting room during the Qing dynasty. Last is the Lamaist **Temple of Eternal Peace – Yong Ansi**. When you emerge at the north side of the island, you'll be facing an elegant marble bridge connecting the island to the shore. From here you can see (or cross over the bridge to visit) the **Round City, Tuancheng** (open daily 8.30am–4.30pm), centre of the Mongol capital of Dadu in the 15th century.

For dinner, the **Fangshan Restaurant** (open daily 11am–1.30pm, 5–7.30pm) is definitely worth the walk around the perimeter of the island. Try the sculpted tofu with vegetables or birds' nest soup. The latter is not a bunch of sticks but a delicacy made from the salivary mucus of the swallow (and tastes much better than it sounds). Leave Beihai Park by the south gate, where taxis wait.

Evening Itineraries

7. Peking Duck and Peking Opera

A classic night on the town. Indulge in the ritual of Peking roast duck and then proceed to the Peking Opera.

– Get to Tiananmen Square. Zhengyangmen Quanjude Roast Duck Restaurant is on the east side, just opposite the Monument to the Heroes of the People. Call ahead for reservations if you have a large group (Tel: 524-0612; open daily noon–1.30pm, 4.30–9.30pm) –

The earliest mention of Peking duck can be traced back to a 12th-century cookbook. The chefs from **Zhengyangmen Quanjude Roast Duck Restaurant** are schooled by Beijing's Quanjude masters, whose predecessors opened the famous Qianmen Quanjude Restaurant just a few blocks to the south in 1864.

To prepare the ambrosial Peking duck, the unfortunate bird's unbroken skin is inflated like a balloon, filled with water and glazed with sugar. The duck is then roasted in an oven heated by burning the wood of fruit

trees such as date, peach and pear. This is done in order to impart a sweet, earthy aroma to the skin and flesh of the bird. When cooked, the skin, now crisp, is sliced into bite-sized pieces and served with a thin pancake, fresh scallions and a salty hoisin bean sauce. The rest of the duck meat is used to cook other dishes accompanying the meal.

Part of the art of this cuisine is to make use of the entire duck, and this restaurant claims to make more than 300 different duck dishes, to be sampled while the duck is roasting. They're much better than they sound. Try the cold mustard duck web, deep-fried duck liver with sesame and the fried duck hearts with chilli sauce, but give the duck soup (à la dishwater) a miss.

When the roast duck arrives, it's your job to finish the preparation on the table, in taco-like fashion. Use your chopsticks to pick up the scallions and use them as a kind of paintbrush to dab some hoisin sauce on the pancake. Add one or two bite-sized pieces of duck, roll it up and viola! This is one of the rare times in China when using your fingers to eat is considered acceptable behaviour, so enjoy it. The cost of a meal at the restaurant is about 40 yuan per person which should include various duck dishes and a drink.

Peking Opera starts at 7.30pm at the **Qianmen Hotel's Liyuan Theatre** (175, Yongan Road), a 10-minute taxi drive from Zhengyangmen (Qianmen). Buy tickets at the booth next to the parking lot.

Peking Opera is so highly stylized that you might think it ancient, but in fact it was created only in the late 18th century, drawing from several regional theatre forms. The result is a feast for the senses, though some foreign viewers may find it a bit hard to swallow. The actors' voices are high and mewing, the face-paint and costumes outrageous, and the action on stage accompanied by a piercing string and percussion ensemble.

In general, Peking operas can be classified into two types of stories – civilian and military. The Qianmen Hotel stages Peking Opera mainly for non-Chinese speaking visitors, so they tend to choose action-packed martial stories, as well as episodes from the classic novel *Journey to the West* – a popular Buddhist epic about the travels of the monk Tripitaka to seek Buddhist scriptures. These are great fun because the characters wear colourful costumes and there are plenty of acrobatics to dramatize battles.

The characters with painted faces called *Jing* are warriors, heroes, statesmen, adventurers and supernatural beings. In general, good guys are painted with

Peking Opera in action

simpler designs while more complicated patterns indicate enemy generals, bandits, robbers and rebels. Colours will tell you if a character is courageous (red), cruel or conniving (oily white), wise (purple) or other-worldly (gold). Some painted designs tell a story, like the suns painted on the face of Hou Yi, the legendary character who shot down nine suns. Aside from the *Jing* there are three main character types: *Dan*, a female lead role traditionally played by a man; *Sheng*, the male lead role; and *Chou*, the clown.

Much can be surmised from the body language of the performers, costumes, movements and props – all of which have set meanings. A single candle might represent evening, while a soldier carrying a banner represents an entire regiment. The hands and body trembling all over indicates extreme anger and a flick of a sleeve expresses disgust. Of course, even the most adept might have some trouble with nuance. There are, for example, at least 20 kinds of laughter, each with slightly different meaning.

Like other traditional arts in China, Peking Opera is slowly losing ground to MTV, Hong Kong and Hollywood movies and karaoke, but there is still a small, dedicated audience who relish this art form.

8. Tiananmen Night Walk

A relaxing sunset walk beginning with the flag-lowering ceremony on Tiananmen Square; then a walk by the moat of the Forbidden City, ending with a visit to the night market and a karaoke bar.

– Take a taxi or pedicab to Tiananmen Square. Bus Nos 2, 10 or 20 and trolley bus Nos 101, 103 or 109 also stop there. This leisurely stroll takes about 45 minutes –

Marching past the state flag

Tiananmen Gate by night

The flag-lowering ceremony happens at sunset, around 7.30pm in summer and 5.30pm in mid-winter. This is one of the few old Soviet-style rituals remaining, similar to the changing of the guard at Lenin's tomb. To encourage patriotism after the Tiananmen crackdown, the ceremony was beefed up with more soldiers and a new and taller flag pole. Hundreds gather each night to watch the military drill and flag-lowering, although it's hard to know precisely what draws them. A favourite pastime in Beijing is to 'kan rinao', which basically means to 'watch the excitement'. This could be anything from a lovers' quarrel to road construction. At any rate, soon after the flag descends, quiet settles over the square. At night, after the lights come up on the Monument to the Martyrs and Tiananmen Gate, the square seems a very different place.

Begin your walk by crossing under Chang'an Avenue through the pedestrians' tunnel, and then passing under Tiananmen Gate. The long approach from Tiananmen Gate, leading through a central gate to Wumen, entrance to the Forbidden City (Palace Museum), is about 600m (656yds), at which point, you'll be forced to turn. Go right and walk along the perimeter of the Forbidden City, between its high wall and the moat. With just a few bicycles whirring past and lovers whispering from park benches, it's easy to imagine you've been transported to another century.

Red bean porridge for supper

Go right, exit through the side gate and take an immediate left. This road runs between the palace and the moat, so you can't get lost. After 50m (55yds), it turns right, goes straight for another 400m (437yds) and turns left where there is another 50-m (55-yds) stretch. At this point you'll see the East Gate of the Forbidden City on the left. The road bends right and becomes **Donghuamen Night Market**. Here, you'll find some of the cheapest eats in town. Try a bowl of red bean porridge or grilled quail. If you're still foraging for a full meal, you've just wandered into a strip of restaurants largely owned by and catering to over-

Digging into Mongolian hotpot

seas Chinese. There is good seafood and Cantonese fare along both sides of the street. Splurge on the braised shark's fin with creamy crab sauce at the swanky **Hong Kong Food City** (on the right side, you can't miss the neon). Or try Mongolian hotpot at any one of the little private restaurants along this stretch. This is a bargain and usually a safe bet even for weak stomachs. You get raw meat and vegetables and a boiling pot of stock to cook them in. The pleasure's in eating the food you've freshly cooked yourself.

There are many karaoke bars tucked away in the many buildings on this street. Karaoke is just about the hottest entertainment trend here in the last couple of years. Any place where you see an 'OK' sign is very likely to be a karaoke joint. One possibility is the **PDK Yuppie Club** (No 5, Goldfish Lane, Wangfujing, Tel: 513-2504), one block past the food market on the left.

The idea is for you to choose a song (they have a menu including Chinese, English, Japanese hits plus songs for children) and pay a fee, for which you get back-up music and plenty of reverb to smooth over the rough spots. The results are sometimes ear-splitting, but at least it's cathartic for the singer. If after your karaoke session, you're still on the go, walk half a block to the **Rumours Disco** at Palace Hotel (No 8 Goldfish Lane, Tel: 512-8899), where you can twist and shout till 2am.

Karaoke-ing

Excursions

9. The Beach at Beidaihe

A relaxing getaway to the seashore at Beidaihe on the Bohai Sea. This is an overnight trip because of the five-hour train ride.

– The Beijing Train Station is on Huochezhan Lu, south of Chang'an Avenue, 2km (1¼ miles) east of Tiananmen Square. Several trains service Beidaihe every day. Best is the express train, No 11, leaving at 6.30am and arriving at Beidaihe just before noon. The return express, No 12, leaves at 2pm and arrives in Beijing by 7pm. Tickets should be booked a few days in advance to ensure availability. Get your tickets from the Foreigner's Booking Office in the left corner of the main hall of the train station or ask your hotel travel service to buy them for you –

If you've conquered Beijing's temples, or they've conquered you, it may be time for a day on the beach at Beidaihe. It's a well-worn path for Beijing's officials and you'll see plenty of Mao suits and military uniforms rolled up to the knec. The top-level leaders, however, are cloistered away at a private beach south of town. The main beaches are packed during July and August – 'a mountain of people, a sea of people', as the Chinese say. But the beach area is kept remarkably clean by those very same fastidious sweepers you see in Beijing. On the hills overlooking the Bohai Sea are mostly old brick villas with broad verandahs. There is a small boardwalk area with a cluster of cheap seafood restaurants.

Of the hotels that receive foreigners, the best deal is **Beidaihe**

R&R at Beidaihe

Beach vendor

Guesthouse for Diplomatic Missions, five minutes' walk from the main beach (No 1 Baosan Lu, Tel: 0335-441 807, or 532-4336 in Beijing). It has friendly, English-speaking staff and a good seafood restaurant. All its rooms have balconies facing the sea. At the high end is the **Jinshan Guesthouse**, (No 4 Dongsan Lu, Tel: 441-338). It's on a quiet beach 4km (2½ miles) north of town, with a business centre, bowling alley, the works. For dinner, go to the outdoor market on Shitang Lu for fresh (and cheap) seafood.

10. Chengde

An overnight stay in Chengde, the eclectic mountain retreat of the Qing Emperors.

– The best way to get to Chengde, 250km (155 miles) north of Beijing, is a five-hour train ride. Buy your tickets from the Foreigners Booking Office, in the left corner of the main hall of the Beijing Train Station within three days of departure, or have your hotel purchase tickets for a small fee. No 11 leaves at 7am and arrives in Chengde at noon. When leaving, the No 12 departs Chengde at 2.30pm, arriving in Beijing at 7.15pm. The train station in Chengde is located on the south side of town. Taxis, three-wheeled motorcycle taxis or bus Nos 2, 3 and 5 will take you to the Guesthouse for Diplomatic Missions, the Yunshan Hotel or the Palace Hotel. By transferring to No 6, you can take the public bus to the Yert Holiday Inn Hotel –

Emperor Kangxi of the Qing dynasty was drawn to the town of Jehol – as Chengde was called in the early 18th century – because of its location in a cool basin, 350m (1,148ft) above sea level and surrounded by mountains, lush forests and placid lakes. He ordered the building of Bishushanzhuang, which means 'Mountain Manor for Escaping the Summer Heat', in 1703. The residence was used throughout the last days of the Qing Dynasty. Emperor Qianlong expanded the residence, incorporating the

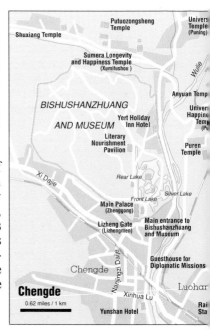

styles of China's minorities in his sprawling kingdom as part of an effort to appease them. In the Yanshan mountains which surround the manor were 11 temples, also varying in architectural styles. Now renovated, **Bishushanzhuang** (open daily 5.30am–6.30pm) is again an excellent escape and a magical place to explore.

If you have just one day in Chengde, spend the first afternoon strolling through Bishushanzhuang and save the more strenuous temple-crawling for the following morning. If you have more time to spare, there are bizarre rock formations, caves and hot springs in the outlying areas. Chengde is quite compact and Bishushanzhuang can be easily reached on foot from the hotels. Otherwise, public buses and van Nos 2, 3 and 5 run straight up the main road, Wulie Jie, and stop next to the main gate of Bishushanzhuang.

Tower of Mist and Rain, Bishushanzhuang

Little in Chengde is translated for non-Chinese speakers. You may want to hire a guide through the local branch of the China International Travel Service (CITS) at Tel: 226-827.

Just inside the main gate is the **Bishushanzhuang Museum** (open daily 8am–5pm) which once housed the main palace. This complex is downright rustic for a palace. Though laid out in the traditional linear style of halls and courtyards, it is made of unpainted wood and shaded by tall pines. The exhibits are varied: some rooms display items such as Mongolian weapons and dress, other rooms are set up as they were when they were used by the royals. Leaving by the back door of the museum takes you to the park proper. This park, surrounded by a 10-km (6½-mile) long wall, is the largest surviving royal garden in China, about twice the size of the Summer Palace in Beijing.

Off to the right, about 100m (109yds), begins a maze of paths, bridges, pavilions and halls surrounding several interlocking lakes. This area is for strolling, renting boats or gazing from park benches. Beyond it is the **Literary Nourishment Pavilion**, one of four imperial libraries. Its central attraction is a rock garden where there is a place to view the moon, a sliver of light perpetually reflected in the pond because of the rock formations. At the far end of the east side of the park, you'll find a meadow marked by the pagoda of the **Temple of Eternal Blessing**, which was

Temple of Eternal Blessing

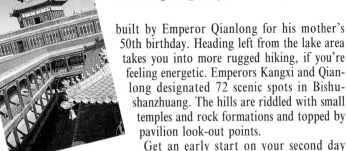

Putuozongsheng Temple

built by Emperor Qianlong for his mother's 50th birthday. Heading left from the lake area takes you into more rugged hiking, if you're feeling energetic. Emperors Kangxi and Qianlong designated 72 scenic spots in Bishushanzhuang. The hills are riddled with small temples and rock formations and topped by pavilion look-out points.

Get an early start on your second day and head for the temples (open daily 8am–5pm) beyond the walls of Bishushanzhuang. The best way to do this is to hire a taxi for the morning or day. Drivers know the circuit, but bring a tourist map. The temple tour would also make a strenuous but pleasant bike ride covering about 25km (15½ miles). There's a bike rental shop about 100m (109yds) north of Yunshan Hotel.

There are eight temples, but start with these four and then see how time and energy hold out. **Putuozongsheng** is the largest and most spectacular complex– a cousin of the Potala in Lhasa. But don't be misled into thinking that the mini-Potala is small: it covers 22ha (54 acres). The 1767 structure is now beautifully restored so that every gold roof gleams in the sun. Prayer flags, banners and tapestries hang from it, Tibetan-style. The design of **Xumishoufu (Sumera Longevity and Happiness) Temple**, just 1km (½ miles) to the east, is based on another Tibetan temple. This temple, built in

1779, is currently being restored. At its rear is an octagonal pagoda commemorating the 70th birthday of Emperor Qianlong.

Puning (Universal Peace) Temple, built in 1755 and 3km (2 miles) farther northeast, is outstanding because it is a living monastery with about 50 lamas in residence. Take a look at the second hall, which is laid out with long, low benches for religious study and ceremony, and a statue of Guanyin, the Goddess of Mercy with a Thousand Hands and a Thousand Eyes. The two characters on

Puning Temple

either side are her disciples. Finally, trek to **Pule (Universal Happiness) Temple**, which lies due east of Bishushanzhuang. It has a distinctly Han Chinese shape, a conical, two-tiered roof similar to that of the Temple of Heaven in Beijing. The great attraction here are the bronze images of the deities in various acts of passionate embrace and conquest of their enemies. These are great examples of the lovely and terrifying imagery that comes with Tibetan Buddhism.

One of the weirdest looking rock formations in the area is **Club Peak**. You can get to it and get an overview of the area by getting on a cable car that starts just a few hundred metres north of Pule Temple: it takes 20 minutes each way.

Chengde as a town is nothing to get excited about. Places to stay range from pretty good – the Yunshan Hotel (No 6 Nanyuan Jie, Dong Lu, Tel: 496-171) and the Chengde Guesthouse for Diplomatic Missions (Wulie Jie, Central Section, Tel: 221-970) to the seedy Palace Hotel (No 21 Wulie Jie, Tel: 225-092). The zaniest option, if you're there between March and October, is the Yert Holiday Inn, located inside Bishushanzhuang, in the northwest corner. You stay in Mongolian tents called *yerts*. It's not exactly camping as the *yerts* are air-conditioned and have individual baths and television, but it's fun.

Local cuisine centres on mainly wild game because this area is on the edge of the Mongolian hunting grounds. Try **Huanggong Yushanfang** (open daily 11am–2pm, 4.30–9pm), the restaurant attached to the Palace Hotel. Girls dressed as Qing dynasty maids serve up venison, wild boar and pheasant. Be sure to ask prices in advance as they're not listed on the menu and you could be surprised.

Mongolian-style yerts

This is a town where staying in your hotel for meals is generally not a bad idea; there are snack vendors but not many clean restaurants near the temples or Bishushanzhuang.

However, there is a funky privately-owned place called **Zhuangyuan Jiudian** (Caoshi Jie, Tel: 222-090; open daily 5pm–midnight) that has just opened. It's clean and cheap and turns into a karaoke or dance floor at about 10pm. As a back-up, there's always the coffeeshop in the Yunshan Hotel (open daily 7am–10pm).

Shopping

Forget any notion you had about an austere workers' paradise. Consumerism is the only meaningful 'ism' around Beijing these days. The number of '*dakuan*' – the fat cats with portable phones – is exploding. Russian traders are flooding into Beijing for goods, and more and more average folks have hard cash instead of the grain coupons they once held. New markets and stores are sprouting up everywhere.

'Socialism with Chinese characteristics', as the government calls its Byzantine economy, has its own rules. It's advisable to check prices first at State stores before you buy a similar item in a hotel shop or the free market. In the free market, bargain, bargain, bargain. Be stubborn, but friendly if you're interested in an item. Avoid drawn out dickering if you're not. Fortunately, China's dual currency system of FEC (Foreign Exchange Certificates) and RMB (Renminbi) has been abolished, leaving only RMB and RMB prices. Still, RMB is not perfectly convertible to foreign currency, thus a black market lingers. If you change money on the black market – an illegal but common practice – avoid street urchins hissing 'chain-gee ma-knee'. Instead, try asking a nice elderly lady in a fixed stall at the free market.

Bargaining usually begins with the shopkeeper suggesting a price and the buyer respond-

Silk Alley shopping

ing with a lower one. In Beijing, the starting price is generally 30–40 percent higher than the price shopkeepers will accept. Of course, if you're buying several things from one shop, you should get a better deal. The main thing is to be persistent, look for missing buttons, stains and other flaws, and keep smiling and walk away if you find the price unacceptable.

Speciality Markets

If shopping is your favourite sport, you'll be in good company in Beijing's bustling markets. **Silk Alley**, or **Xiushui Shichang** on Xuishiu Jie which intersects with Chang'an Avenue about 800m (872yds) east of the Friendship Store, has been growing in the last two years and now threatens to overtake the neighbouring diplomatic area. As the name implies, vendors flog silk in all shapes and sizes – ties and boxer shorts, dresses and slinky nightgowns – at prices about half of Hong Kong's. Just a few blocks away at Ritan Lu, opposite Ritan Park is **Yabaolu Market** (open daily 9am–6pm), another huge and growing clothing market specializing in cotton and wool garments and goose down jackets.

A few blocks straight north of Yabaolu Market is the **Chaowai Flea Market** (open daily 10am–6pm), located off Third Ring Road at Jingdong east intersection, a favourite stomping ground for resident diplomats and journalists. The front building is filled with antique and classical-style furniture. In the rear building are curios – snuff bottles, ceramics and Mao memorabilia. There's lots more where this comes from. **Hongqiao Farmers' Market** at Tiantan Lu (open daily 7am–5.30pm) has the best collection of antique clocks and Mao statues, as well as reams of freshwater pearls (see *Pick & Mix 1*).

For traditional Chinese paintings, calligraphy supplies and rare books, poke around at **Liulichang** (open daily 9am–5.30pm), just west of Qianmen district (see *Pick & Mix 2*). A bit further

Liulichang for books

afield, but considered to be the most reliable source of antique porcelain in Beijing is **Jingsong Market** (open daily 9am–6pm) located at East Third Ring Road at the Jingsong east intersection.

Antiques that date from before 1795 may not be exported legally. Those which can be taken out of China must carry a small red seal

Bird Market vendor

or have one affixed by the Cultural Relics Bureau. Beware of fakes; producing new 'antiques' (and the seal) is a thriving industry here.

Tucked under the southeast corner of the Xizhimen overpass, the **Bird Market** (open daily 7.30am–sunset) is hardly an extension of nature, but it has a wonderful array of feathered creatures. At least as important are the elegant handmade cages, ceramic feeders and other bird paraphernalia sold here. The bird market is one part shopping, one part hobnobbing.

Non-Tourist Shopping Spots

There are three lively shopping streets in the city centre which cater to local customers. **Wangfujing**, **Xidan** and **Dongdan**, which run perpendicular to Chang'an Avenue, have traditionally sold mostly inexpensive local goods, with bargains on leather and furs.

At 192 Wangfujing Dajie, check out the **Jianhua Leather Goods Company** (open daily 8am–8.30pm). It covers the range – leather jackets for as little as 250 yuan to full-length mink coats running up to 18,000 yuan. You'll also find suede backpacks, belts and fox pelts.

Further north, along the east side of Wangfujing is the **Foreign Languages Bookstore**, run by the China News Agency. The first floor has a wide range of books on China. The floor upstairs is off limits to foreigners though as it is stuffed full of pirated copies for Chinese customers.

CIVIC-Yaohan for luxury imports

All three streets are undergoing radical transformation, with more and more boutiques, watch stores and ice-cream shops replacing the old standbys. Xidan and Wangfujing are both slated for massive rebuilding which will expand the shopping greatly.

Among the most popular department stores for Chinese products is **Longfu Dasha** (No 95 Longfusi Jie, Chaoyang District; open daily 8.30am–8.30pm). This is the spot to buy China's most famous brands of household products, such as Flying Pigeon bicycles and Butterfly sewing machines.

Palace Hotel designer row

One-stop shopping

Capitalism's answer for one-stop shoppers is in the shape of glossy, new joint venture shopping centres that draw China's nouveau riche as well as tourists and mobs of window shoppers. Directly across the street from the Friendship Store is the **CIVIC-Yaohan** (No 22 Jianguomenwai Dajie, open daily 9am–9pm), a Japanese department store chock-full of luxury imports like Gucci handbags at 3,000 yuan apiece.

The **Youyi Shopping City** (No 52 Liangmaqiao Lu, Chaoyang District; open daily 9am–9pm) which opened in 1992 at the Beijing Lufthansa Centre, carries products with a broader price range. The city's best selection of silks by the yard are sold at reasonable prices here.

Most large hotels have shops. The lobby and basement levels of the Palace Hotel cater to brand-name hunters. Monde, Celine, Louis Vuitton and Pierre Cardin all have stores here – a symbol of the new spending power in China. At the Hong Kong lingerie boutique, La Perla, women are snapping up Italian bras for as much as US$150.

Stock up on all the beautiful things that China produces, like traditional paper cuttings (cheap and easy to pack), jade carvings, kites and chopsticks at the state-run **Friendship Store** (No 17 Jianguomenwai Dajie; open daily 9am–9pm). The store is also good for getting an estimate of what things outside should cost, and for any last-minute gifts.

Eating Out

In China, when people greet each other on the street, instead of inquiring 'How are you?' they ask, 'Have you eaten?' Food is an obsession in China, perhaps harkening back to the day not too long ago when people didn't get enough of it. Whatever the reason, the culinary arts are highly valued and varied. The range of eating options is enormous, from street vendors that serve up grilled yams for 1 yuan to foreign restaurants dishing out meals that would gobble up the average local person's monthly income. For the tourist, Beijing offers the opportunity to taste dishes from all over China at reasonable prices. Hotels and new western restaurants also serve a wide range of cuisines for the homesick palate. Note that many State-run restaurants stop serving dinner by 7.30pm.

The approximate cost of a meal for one person is categorized thus: $=10–75 yuan; $$=75–150 yuan; $$$=more than 150 yuan.

Chinese

Beijing and Imperial Cuisine

Many dishes classified as Peking-style were originally gleaned from

Jianbing vendor

all over the kingdom, perfected and embellished in the Imperial Court. Beijing cuisine makes liberal use of strongly-flavoured roots and vegetables like peppers, garlic, ginger, leek and coriander. The dishes of the north tend to be heartier, with noodles and steamed or fried breads as the staple, rather than rice.

Jianbing, commonly sold by street vendors, is certainly Beijing's most popular (or at least most widely sold) street food. It is a combination of eggs and scallions whipped up on a hot griddle and sandwiched between a kind of deep-fried cracker, often along with *youtiao* (deep-fried dough sticks). It is then slathered in a hot peppery sauce. The most famous northern dish is Peking duck, which is in fact a whole meal using all the different parts of the duck.

FANGSHAN CANTING
Qionghua Dao
Beihai Park
Tel: 401-1889
Garden setting at Beihai Park. *$$*

LI FAMILY RESTAURANT
11 Yongfang Hutong
Denei Dajie
Tel: 601-1915
Serves four tables of up to 12 each day – two at lunch and two at dinner in the home of the chef, who has a story for each dish. Book ahead. *$$*

Peking Duck Restaurants

ZHENGYANGMEN QUANJUDE ROAST DUCK RESTAURANT
East side of Tiananmen Square, opposite War Heroes Monument
Tel: 512-2265
Clean and well-run, with more than 300 different duck dishes. *$*

QIANMEN QUANJUDE ROAST DUCK RESTAURANT
32 Qianmen Dajie
Tel: 511-2418

Beijing's most famous. The restaurant is arranged so you can watch the duck being prepared. *$$*

Shandong Cuisine

Dishes from neighbouring Shandong Province are the main element in what Beijingers refer to as home cooking. The number of restaurants serving this fare outnumber any other kind. Because Shandong is a coastal province, its dishes feature seafood such as jumbo shrimp, eel, sharks' fin and sea cucumber.

SPECIAL FLAVOURS RESTAURANT
7/F Beijing Hotel, Old West Wing
33 East Chang'an Avenue
Tel: 513-7766, ext 374
Dine in a classic Chinese banquet room. *$$*

CONFUCIAN HERITAGE RESTAURANT
3 West Liulichang Jie
Tel: 303-0689
An inviting two-storey teahouse in the historical Liulichang area. *$–$$*

Sichuan Cuisine

The isolated southwestern province of Sichuan is known for its spicy food, which, it is said, matches the temperament of the people. Chicken, pork, freshwater fish and shellfish are favourite ingredients, and noodles or bread is usually served as the staple. Try some wicked *dan dan* noodles or a sizzling fish-head soup.

Roast duck meal

many excellent Cantonese restaurants in Beijing, but they also tend to be more expensive than other Chinese restaurants.

WINDOWS ON THE WORLD
28/F, CITIC Building
19 Jianguomenwai Dajie
Tel: 500-3335
Excellent *dim sum* dishes served in a pleasant dining room on the 28th floor, overlooking the west of the city. *$$*

FOUR SEASONS
1/F Jianguo Hotel
Jianguomenwai Dajie
Tel: 500-2233, ext 8041
Quiet, classical setting enhances the fine food. *$$*

HONG KONG FOOD CITY
18 Dong'anmen Dajie
Tel: 513-6668
Fresh seafood served in a lively dining hall. *$$*

Other Chinese Restaurants

BAMBOO GARDEN HOTEL RESTAURANT
24 Xiaoshiqiao
Jiugulou Street
Tel: 403-2229
Hearty Chinese dishes served in a classical garden restaurant. Formerly the home of a shadowy secret security chief, Kang Sheng. *$*

KAOROUJI RESTAURANT
14 Qianhai Dongyan
Tel: 401-2170/445-921
Muslim-style grill on Qianhai Lake. *$*

XINJIANG RESTAURANTS
Weiguncun Uyghur Village
off Baishiqiao Road
Pick any restaurant in this three-block area for noodles and grilled mutton made by Uighur people. *$*

SICHUAN RESTAURANT
51 Xi Rongxian Hutong
Tel: 603-3291
Frequented by some of Beijing's leaders. Located in what was the mansion of a Qing dynasty prince. *$*

RITAN RESTAURANT
Southwest corner of Ritan Park
Tel: 500-4984
Indoor and courtyard dining in the Temple of the Sun Park. Live traditional music in the summer. *$*

YIDAIREN HOME MADE FOOD
181 Xi'anmen Dajie
(opposite the Honglou Cinema)
Tel: 601-5097
Cozy and clean, privately-owned restaurant with cooks straight from Sichuan Province. *$*

Cantonese Cuisine
Cantonese food is known for its delicate flavours and fresh ingredients, preferably bought the same day and cooked briskly before serving, using little oil or spicy seasoning. *Dim sum* are dumplings meant to be a snack food, but there are so many different kinds to try that a *dim sum* meal often turns into a feast. There are now

DONGLAISHUN RESTAURANT
(2 branches)
16 Jinyu Hutong and
198 Wangfujing Dajie
Tel: 552-2092/550-069/556-465
Mongolian hotpot. *$*

DUYICHU DUMPLING SHOP
36 Qianmen Dajie
Tel: 511-2094
A Beijing tradition. *$*

Other Asian Cuisines

OMAR KHAYYAM
Asia Pacific Building
8 Yabao Lu
Tel: 513-9988, ext 20188
Tasty Indian cuisine in pleasant surroundings. *$$*

SAKURA
2F Changfugong New Otani Hotel
Jianguomenwai Dajie
Tel: 512-5555, ext 1226
Japanese. Light and sunny atmosphere. $$

GO NIN NYAKUSHOU
2/F Beijing Hotel
East Chang'an Avenue
Tel: 513-7766, ext 666
Japanese food and posh ambience. *$$$*

LIYUAN RESTAURANT
8 Xi Huangchenggen
Tel: 601-5234
Thai and Chinese food. *$$*

Western

PAULANER BRAUHAUS
Beijing Lufthansa Centre
50 Liangmaqiao Lu
Tel: 465-3388, ext 5734
Friendly pub serving tasty German fare. The beer is brewed in-house. *$$*

FRANK'S PLACE
Gongrentiyuguan Donglu
(next to Chains City Hotel)
Tel: 507-2617
All-American venture with the best burger and chilli in town. Darts and re-runs of the National Football League add to the fun atmosphere. *$*

MAXIM'S
(2 branches)
2 Chongwenmennei Dajie
Tel: 512-1992 and
West Wing, China World Trade Centre
Tel: 505-4853
French restaurant, modelled after Maxim's of Paris. Owned by couturier Pierre Cardin. *$$*

LA FLEUR
3/F China World Hotel
1 Jianguomenwai Dajie
Tel: 505-2266
Elegant French nouvelle cuisine. *$$$*

PEPPINO'S
Shangri-La Hotel
29 Zizhuyuan Lu
Tel: 841-2211
Romantic Italian restaurant. Candlelight dinners and a roving guitarist. *$$*

PRIME CUT
37/F China World Hotel
1 Jianguomenwai Dajie
Tel: 505-2266, ext 6549
Steaks American-style with a great view of the city. *$$*

Chefs at Paulaner Brauhaus

Nightlife

'Beijing nightlife' was once a contradiction in terms, but as China opens up and its people have more time and money for leisure, even the puritanical capital is beginning to shake. A little. Some of the traditional forms of amusement – the teahouse and the night market, for example – are coming back to life. And new forms of entertainment, especially jazz shows and discos, are catching on. But it's still a trick knowing where to look for what.

If you're interested in doing as the Beijingers do, then the first place to go is where the food is – night markets and private restaurants. Night markets are fair weather spots where you can sit outside, eat snacks and swill cool beer. When the weather's cold, seek out Mongolian hotpot, which both cooks your dinner and keeps your hands warm. Ballroom dancing made a powerful comeback in the 1980s and remains popular. There are many parks and private dance halls that offer a chance to dust off your foxtrot, normally with no pain to the wallet. Karaoke has taken China by storm. Some of Beijing's better known ones are listed here, but any place that has the telltale 'OK' on the sign is a fair bet. Theatres are plentiful, but good movies are not; in fact, China's best films are nearly always shown abroad before they're approved for audiences here.

The most dramatic change is in the realm of music. Discos have proliferated and major hotels are beefing up their live offerings with local and overseas acts. Several local entrepreneurs have started rock-n-roll clubs, but these are ephemeral. Ask long-term foreign residents to tell you about the latest on that front. Apart from the following nightlife suggestions, be sure to check the English-language paper, *Beijing Weekend* and the glossy tourism publication, *Welcome to China*, available at most hotels.

Beijing is still a casual place. Formal dress is not required anywhere, though neatness is appreciated. Beijing, for its size, is still amazingly safe, but take heed: men alone or in groups should be wary of enticing little bars with hostesses who join you for a drink. The price for the company is usually astronomically high, and there are enforcers to make sure you pay.

Night Markets

LOTUS FLOWER MARKET
Southwest shore of Qianhai Lake
Authentic Beijing-style local night market with great atmosphere. Closes about midnight.

DONGHUAMEN MARKET
One block West of Palace Hotel
Beijing snacks plus lamb kebabs and Cantonese sweets. Closes about 10pm.

SNACK CITY (XIAOCHICHENG)
Courtyard next to the Peace Hotel
Set up with tourists in mind. Clean and cheap. Closes about 11pm.

CHANGLIANG 'EVERBRIGHT' NIGHT PLAZA
Between the Great Wall Sheraton Hotel and Landmark Towers
A carnival-like approach to traditional snacks, with late-night shopping alongside. Open 8 April–8 October, 6pm–midnight, closed Monday.

Ballroom Dancing

YUE LI YUAN FLOWER GARDEN
Ditan Park
Live band with music ranging from disco to waltz. Good clean fun. Open 7.30–9.30pm.

ZHONGSHAN PARK
Enter from Chang'an Avenue, just west of Tiananmen Gate
Tel: 605-5439
Indoor and outdoor dance floors. Open 7.30–10.30pm.

Lotus Flower Market vendor

Live Music

ALFRED'S
Sara Hotel
2 Wangfujing Dajie
Tel: 513-6666
Tex-Mex setting with a variety of live performers playing anything from cool jazz to local rock and roll. No cover. Open until 3am.

MAXIM'S
West Building
China World Trade Centre
Jianguomenwai Dajie
Tel: 505-4853

Restaurant owned by Pierre Cardin is roaring 20s retro. Live jazz band on Friday/Saturday nights till midnight.

MAXIM'S
(Beijing's original)
2 Chongwenmen Xidajie
Tel: 512-1992
Jazz every night except the last Saturday of the month, when there's live rock-n-roll instead. Open from 11.30am–2.30pm, 4.30pm–midnight.

Brauhaus brouhaha

RED LION BAR
37/F China World Trade Centre
1 Jianguomenwai Dajie
Tel: 505-2266, ext 6548
English-style pub with regular piano jazz performances by candlelight. Excellent view of the city is a bonus. A civilized place for a nightcap. Open 9pm–midnight.

Pubs/Bars

BRAUHAUS
1/F China World Trade Centre
1 Jianguomenwai Dajie
Tel: 505-2266, ext 6565
A noisy, crowded and friendly place to mix with Beijing's long-termers. Open 11am–2am.

FRANK'S PLACE
Gongrentiyuguan Donglu
Tel: 507-2617

All American watering hole with NFL re-runs and darts. Open 12–2pm, 5pm–1am.

MEXICAN WAVE
45 Dongdaqiao Lu
Tel: 506-2222
Serves Mexican food and lots of beer. A wild one. Open 11am until the last person leaves.

Karaoke

PDK YUPPIE CLUB
5 Goldfish Lane
Wangfujing
Tel: 513-2504
Karaoke extraordinaire. Private rooms available for parties, with songs in Mandarin, English, Cantonese, Japanese and Taiwanese, including tunes for the kids. Open 8pm–2am.

Frank's Place

Chaoyang acrobats

EDEN CLUB
3/F Polyplaza Building
Gongrentiyuguanlu and
Chaoyangmen Beidajie
Tel: 500-1188
Glitzy disco and karaoke popular
with Chinese entrepreneurs. Open
8pm–3am.

DYNASTY KARAOKE AND PIANO BAR
1/F Sara Hotel
2 Wangfujing Dajie
Tel: 513-6666
Open 8pm–3am.

Discos

HOUSE
3 Goldfish Lane
Wangfujing
Tel: 512-8833, ext 6622
A wild one, especially popular with
visitors from Hong Kong and Taiwan. Open 8.30pm–2.30am.

RUMOURS
Palace Hotel
8 Goldfish Lane, Wangfujing
Open 8pm–2am.

TALK OF THE TOWN
Ground level, China World Hotel
1 Jianguomenwai Dajie
Tel: 505-2266, ext 6126
Open 9pm–2am.

JULIANNA'S
Holiday Inn Lido Hotel
Tel: 437-6688
Thursdays free for ladies. Open
9pm–2am.

Traditional Theatre And Shows

LIYUAN THEATRE
Qianmen Hotel
175 Yongan Road
Tel: 301-6688
Peking opera every night, from
7.30pm. (See *Pick & Mix 7*)

LAO SHE TEAHOUSE
3/F Dawancha Building
3 Qianmen Xi Dajie
Tel: 303-6830
The variety performance features ex-
cerpts from Peking opera, acrobatics,
and comic 'crosstalk'. Open 7.30pm–
9.30pm nightly.

TIANQIAO LE (PARADISE) TEAHOUSE
60 Tianqiao Market
Beiwei Lu
Tel: 304-0617
Old Peking teahouse with shows fea-
turing acrobats, traditional music,
comic sketches and 'feats of strength'.
Ticket include snacks and tea.

CHAOYANG THEATRE
36 Dongsanhuan Beilu
Tel: 507-2421
Those amazing Chinese acrobats. Every night at 7.15pm.

Fashion show, Julianna's

Calendar of Special Events

Whenever you arrive in China, it will be close to an official holiday or traditional festival. Holidays such as National Day and International Labour Day are fixed on the modern calendar, but most traditional festivals and events are determined by the lunar calendar, which means that the date varies a little from year to year. Precise dates for these celebrations and information on annual events, such as the Beijing Marathon, can be obtained through the Beijing branch of the China International Travel Service (CITS) located at Tourism Building, No 28 Jianguomenwai Dajie, Tel: 515-8570.

Spring Festival celebrations

JANUARY / FEBRUARY

The new calender year begins with the tolling of the bell at Big Bell Temple (Dazhongsi) and a one-day public holiday. But the biggest bash is dur-

Longtanhu fair during the Spring Festival

ing Lunar New Year, called **Chinese New Year** or **Spring Festival**, which falls in late January or early February. As winter wears on, public buildings are festooned with coloured lights, people from all over China travel to unite with their families, debts are settled, and there is food – lots of it. In northern China, a boiled dumpling called *jiaozi* is a holiday staple – both eating them and gathering to make them. At midnight on the eve of the Chinese New Year,

Longqingxia Ice Lantern Festival

fireworks still explode throughout the city (in defiance of a recent ban) and the bell is rung in the Bell Tower. On the first days of the lunar year, Chinese people put on their Sunday best and go visiting family and friends. In recent years, a more relaxed atmosphere has brought the revival of old Spring Festival traditions, such as giving *hongbao* – little red envelopes containing money – to children and young adults. Temple fairs at Longtanhu and Ditan Parks throughout January and February feature martial arts shows, stand-up comic sketches called 'crosstalk', home-made toys and, of course, more food.

At the same time, Longqingxia Park in the suburbs of Beijing holds its annual **Ice Lantern Festival**. During this several-weeks-long event, organizations and companies sponsor the construction of an ice city, complete with palaces, gigantic ice slides and grandiose sculptures which glow with coloured lights.

Northerners, who have amazing resilience to the bitterly cold winters, partake with gusto in ice-sculpting competitions and winter swimming. The time and duration of the festival depends on the weather.

MARCH / APRIL

March brings a breather for Chinese women. **International Women's Day** on March 8 is an official half-day holiday for the fairer sex.

On the 12th day of the third lunar month, around April 4 or 5, Chinese people honour their deceased relatives by observing **Qingming** – sometimes referred to as the 'grave-sweeping' day. Qingming is a time for mourning, but also for revelling on a warm spring day.

With spring comes the **Beijing International Kite Festival** at the Mentougou Sports Centre, held for five days in mid-April. The tradition dates back 2,500 years. Beijing's master kite-builders show off their traditional dragon kites alongside high-tech stunt flyers from abroad.

In late April and early May the Beijing Botanical Gardens bursts into a riot of colours for the **Peach Blossom Festival**.

MAY / JUNE

International Labour Day is a one-day public holiday. Following hot on its heels is **Youth Day**, a commemora-

National Day Celebrations at Tiananmen

tion of the May 4th Movement of 1919, reflected mainly by large editorials and government hoopla in the official press.

International Children's Day is celebrated in earnest on June 1, by letting out classes early and treating children to an outing at public parks or the zoo.

The crushing of the **Democracy Movement** on June 4th, 1989 is not forgotten either. The occasion is normally marked by the increase of plainclothes policemen positioned around Tiananmen Square and the universities. As a foreigner, you may not be allowed in either place on or just before the 4th.

To beat the dog days of summer, there is now an annual **Watermelon Festival** held in nearby Daxing County, at the tail end of June and first week of July.

JULY / AUGUST

July 1 is the **Anniversary of the Communist Party**, which was founded in Shanghai in 1921. This means very little to the average citizen but plenty of banquets are held for high-level party members.

The fifth day of the fifth lunar month – usually late July – brings the **Dragon Boat Festival**, marked in Beijing by international dragon boat races. The festival has been celebrated from China's earliest times and a number of legends are associated with it. Triangular glutinous rice cakes called *zongzi* used to be thrown into the river where a famous poet is said to have hurled himself overboard. Nowadays, *zongzi* are eaten to mark the occasion. The location of the dragon boat races varies from year to year: check the tourism newspapers

78

or with your hotel information desk.

From late July to early September, Beijing celebrates the **Lantern Festival** at Beihai Park. The Lantern Festival dates back as far as the 9th century BC and is thought to be connected to the lifting of the evening curfew for a few days at this time each year. Elaborate home-made lanterns light up the streets for the occasion. It is traditionally held two weeks into the lunar new year, but for practical reasons – mainly blustery spring winds – Beijing now holds it in late summer.

August 1 is the **Anniversary of the People's Liberation Army**. Inaugurated in 1927 and formerly marked by enormous parades, it is now noted mainly in the media.

SEPTEMBER / OCTOBER

The **Mid-Autumn Festival** again depends on when the moon reaches its fullest, usually around mid-September. The shops do great business in 'moon cakes', pastries filled with gooey sesame paste, red-bean and walnut filling. In the tradition of poets, this is the time to drink a bit of wine and toast the moon.

Late September is normally the time when Chinese communities celebrate the memory of Confucius. The Confucius Temple (Kong Miao) has just resumed the annual ceremony.

October 1 is the PRC's birthday, **National Day**, celebrated with a two-day public holiday. Five- and 10-year anniversaries have been accompanied in the past by grandiose fireworks exhibitions and performances by multitudes of dancers in Tiananmen Square. Other years, government buildings, road intersections and hotels are decked out in lights and flower arrangements and Sun Yat-sen's portrait is displayed in Tiananmen Square. Tens of thousands turn out on the square for picture-taking and general merry-making.

In the third week of October, when the weather is almost always glorious, the city is host to the yearly **Beijing International Marathon**.

NOVEMBER / DECEMBER

November and December are quiet months in China, but **Christmas** is gaining momentum as a celebration for consumers, Christians and curious onlookers. The western churches hold special services which draw thousands of extra spectators. It is now very trendy to exchange greeting cards and presents, while in shopping areas, Santa Claus makes the odd appearance. Most large hotels have special meals and programmes during the Christmas and New Year season. Another way to celebrate the occasion – if you happen to be in China during the winter holidays – is to go ice skating on the lakes, where the mood is perpetually festive.

Ice skating at X'mas

Practical Information

GETTING THERE

By Air

Capital International Airport connects Beijing to all parts of China and to many of the world's major cities. In most cases, you can save money by flying through Hong Kong. Beijing's airport is 27km (25 miles), or a 25-minute drive from the city centre.

Taxis are on the left as you leave the terminal. Air China has a coach service to

its ticket offices at Xidan, west of Tiananmen Square and Dongsi, in the northeast quadrant of the city. This is recommended only if you have light baggage and know where you're going after you get off the bus. Most major hotels offer limousine or bus transfers. Passengers on international arrivals must fill out arrival cards, customs and health declarations. Travellers with active tuberculosis and AIDS carriers are barred from entry.

If you're leaving on a domestic flight from Beijing, check in at least 30 minutes before the flight or you will lose your seat. (29 minutes before the flight is not good enough.) International flight check-in should be done at least one hour be-

fore the flight. Foreigners leaving China by air are required to pay a 90 yuan airport tax. Domestic flight tax is 15 yuan.

By Rail

If you should come via the Trans-Siberian Railway, you will arrive at the main Beijing Train Station in the city centre. This is about 200m (218yds) south of Chang'an Avenue and about 2km (1¼ miles) east of Tiananmen Square. All the same health and customs procedures apply as arriving via an international flight. Taxis are available on the far right-hand side of the parking lot. Beware of taxi drivers who try to shanghai unwitting travellers even before they reach the taxi stand. They usually set outlandish prices.

For train tickets from Beijing to other parts of China, go to the Foreigners' Booking Office in the soft berth waiting room in the far left-hand corner of the Beijing Train Station main hall. Return tickets cannot be purchased at the Beijing station but must be bought in the city of departure.

Tickets for the Trans-Siberian Railway can be purchased at the International Travel and Ticketing Centre at the Beijing International Hotel (No 9 Jianguomenwai Daijie, Tel: 512-0507).

Beijing Train Station

When to Visit

The best season to visit Beijing is in autumn – from early September to late November. It's normally warm or cool, and dry. If you come between March and May, chances are you'll encounter at least one of the annual dust storms that blow off the Gobi Desert. Summers can be blistering and humid. The hottest month, July, averages 25.8°C (78°F) but temperatures occasionally soar to nearly 40°C (104°F). Winters are cold and grey. The coldest month, January, averages -5°C (23°F) but temperatures can drop to -23°C (-9°F). Locals wear several layers of clothing all winter, but fear not – one of the best deals in China is silk thermal underwear.

Visas and Passports

Valid passports and visas are required for all foreign tourists. Visas may be obtained at embassies or consulates of the People's Republic of China, or through overseas offices of the state-run China International Travel Service.

Most group tourists are allowed entry through group visas, which are not inserted into passports. For individual travellers, single entry visas are valid for entry within three months of issue. Business or commercial visas are issued at the airport upon presentation of a letter, fax, or similar document from a Chinese official, organization or company. This group has an easier time getting multiple-entry visas good for six months at a time. Each visa is valid for a stay of 30 or 60 days, and can be extended in China for a small fee at the foreign affairs section of public security bureaus.

Carry your passport with you at all times, as it will often be required for checking into hotels, making reservations, changing money and other bank transactions. If your passport is lost or stolen, contact your embassy immediately and the Foreigners' Section of the Public Security Bureau of Beijing Municipality, at 85 Beichizi Jie, Tel: 555-2729.

Customs

Written declarations are required only for visitors carrying more than US$5,000, or exceeding duty-free limits. Chinese customs are especially sensitive to pornographic materials and publications considered anti-government. Airlines flying into China are required to collect all foreign newspapers and magazines before landing to prevent their dissemination, and you may be required to hand in audio and videotapes overnight for inspection. Foreigners carrying illicit drugs have been sentenced to long prison terms. If you arrive in Beijing via the Trans-Siberian Railway, all customs procedures are handled at the Chinese border. All the same rules apply.

Electricity

Electrical current runs at 220 volts. Many hotels have 110-volt shaving sockets.

Time

Beijing time is eight hours ahead of Greenwich Mean Time (GMT).

Geography

Beijing municipality covers 16,808sq km (6,488sq miles). To its south is the North China Plain and to the east is the Bohai Gulf. On the west, northwest and northeast are mountain ranges.

Government and Economy

Beijing is the capital city of the People's Republic of China. It is centre of operations for the Chinese Communist Party (CCP), headed by Jiang Zemin, who is also President. Premier Li Peng is head of government. The country's 3,000-strong legislative body, the People's Congress,

A bustling metropolis

Buddhism, Taoism, Islam and Christianity are all practised in churches, temples and mosques around the city. Proselytizing outside these institutions is forbidden and all religious groups are supposed to be registered with the government. In Beijing, albeit somewhat less than in other parts of China, there are underground (unregistered) Christian groups.

How Not To Offend

China is not a place known for politeness, so there's nothing particularly subtle about its etiquette. Be firm, but remain calm, even if you feel frustrated. Making a public scene engenders resentment and rarely helps get anything done here. Avoid eating with your fingers or licking them.

meet in Beijing yearly. In theory, the congress has the power to approve or reject legislation but it is still widely regarded as a rubber stamp parliament. Personal connections and bureaucracy are still the main operating forces within the government.

Beijing is one of three municipalities (along with Shanghai and Tianjin) with status equal to that of China's provinces. It is divided into 10 administrative districts. The local government set-up mirrors that of the central government. The government is led by the Communist Party, with limited participation by non-CCP officials.

China's economy is in transition from socialism to a 'socialist market economy'. Beijing was well behind the southern and coastal cities in encouraging capitalism, but is quickly catching up. State stores are contracting out space to private vendors and workers are leaving their old workplaces to become entrepreneurs. Places like banks and post offices are still in the grips of the old system. The new system is especially evident in the large and growing number of privately-run restaurants.

Religion

For most of Communist rule, worship of all kinds was discouraged or actively suppressed in China. Since 1979, there has been a revival of the main religions, but society is largely areligious. However,

Population

Beijing has a population of 11 million making it the second largest city after Shanghai. The majority Han people make up nearly 97 percent of the total population. Of the 300,000 minority people in Beijing, about half are Muslims.

MONEY MATTERS

Currency

China has recently boiled down its dual currency system to a single currency making life easier for visitors. All prices are now measured in renminbi yuan (RMB or 'people's currency'. Hotel rates are often cited in US dollars, but are paid in

RMB according to the current rate. Hard currency can be changed for RMB at banks, the Friendship Store and large hotels.

Chinese money is counted in yuan, jiao, and fen. One yuan is 100 fen or 10 jiao. One jiao is 10 fen. The jiao is also called a mao, colloquially. Bills are denominated in 10, 20 and 50 fen notes, and 1, 5, 10, 50 and 100 yuan notes. There are new 1 yuan coins. There are also 1, 2 and 5 fen coins which are almost worthless.

Credit Cards

Major credit cards like Diner's Club, Federal Card, American Express, Master-Card, Visa and JCB are accepted at all but low-budget hotels. Restaurants and stores geared toward tourism also accept them, but large department stores that serve mainly Chinese customers do not. Credit cards can also be used at banks in Beijing to get foreign currency for a small service fee.

Money Changers/Black Market

Since the elimination of the second currency – FEC, or Foreign Exchange Certificates – which had an artificially high value, black market foreign exchange activity has diminished considerably. However, since the RMB is still not perfectly convertible and accessible, there is still a black market for foreign currency. It is technically illegal for most businesses to conduct foreign currency transactions, but in some markets you may get a favourable price with your franc, mark or dollar. Vendors may also approach you to change money at a rate slightly higher than the official one, though this is also illegal. Again, if you choose to do this, avoid money changers who you don't know or who are not obviously connected with a shop. They are very good at sleight-of-hand rip-offs. If you happen to receive FEC in a transaction, don't worry; it is still legal currency, although is gradually being removed from circulation.

When you change money at authorized currency exchange points, be sure to save your receipts. You'll need them as proof of your original purchase if you want to change RMB back to hard currency as you leave the country.

Price Differences

At most major sites, entrance fees for foreigners are several times higher than for locals. In fact, some maintain a three-tiered system that distinguishes between local Chinese, overseas Chinese and other foreigners. There's nothing you can do about this, but when you're buying snacks or drinks from vendors, you can insist on the same price locals are paying.

Tipping

In Chairman Mao's time, tipping was thought of as a bourgeois affectation. For better or worse, some hotel staff have come to expect tips, especially bell boys and restroom attendants. It is not necessary to tip taxi drivers or doormen.

Restaurants catering to foreigners usually add a 10 or 15 percent service charge to the bill. You may want to leave additional small change if you have received exceptional service.

GETTING AROUND

Taxis

Taxis are plentiful and operate on a meter system. Cheapest are the little yellow mini-vans at 1 yuan per kilometre, with a flag-down rate of 10 yuan. Smaller cars cost 1.6 yuan per kilometre; flag-down rate is 10.40 yuan. Sedans are 2 yuan per kilometre; flag-down rate is 12 yuan.

Few taxi drivers speak English so it is a good idea to carry the name and address of your hotel and all your destinations written out in Chinese before heading off. Drivers are required to post their car number and picture identification inside the cab. You may want to note the car number in case of complaints.

Beijing's taxi drivers are generally honest. Do not be alarmed unduly if they

take convoluted routes. The city's many one-way streets and complex traffic rules forbid left turns at many intersections. Small tips are appreciated, though not essential. Be forewarned that drivers who line up for hours in front of hotels are hoping for big fares.

Bus

Beijing's intricate and changing bus network can be a mystery even to lifetime residents of the city. Public buses pack in passengers like sardines during the rush hour. However, buses can be convenient for short distances down main avenues. Hop on and buy your ticket from the roving ticket clerk on board. Cost is 50 fen or less, depending on distance.

Subway

Beijing's subway system is a cheap way to get to the general vicinity of your destination; just 50 fen to go anywhere in the system. Buy your ticket when you enter the subway station. It gets crowded during rush hour, but is generally more civilized than the bus. A conductor announces stops in Chinese and English.

Car

Rental cars come with drivers and can be hired from most hotels. Negotiate for half- and whole-day rates.

Bicycles

Bicycles can be rented at most of the major hotels by hotel guests. There is a bicycle rental and repair shop directly across the street from the Friendship Hotel. Also, the centrally-located Beijing Hotel rents to non-guests. Beijingers ride all year round and through all kinds of weather, even when it snows. For the tourist it's a fun, efficient and eco-friendly way to see the sites in the city.

Pedicabs

Pedicabs are available at some hotels and have set rates. They can also be flagged down (or they'll find you) near most tourist sites. Prices are negotiable and range from about 5 to 30 yuan, depending on the distance and time of day. For example, a ride from the Friendship Store to Tiananmen Square, which is 4km (2½ miles), should cost about 20 yuan. Note that it is often more expensive than taking a mini-van.

Traffic is getting more snarled by the day and the city is riddled with construction sites that cause frequent traffic jams. Getting across town can take 20 minutes or an hour, depending on the time of day. During rush hour, it is better to walk, cycle, or take a pedicab than to take a taxi to nearby destinations.

HOURS AND HOLIDAYS

Business Hours

Business hours vary. Government offices (and this includes banks, domestic ticketing offices, police offices and the like) are generally open 9am–5pm (and some only until 4.30pm) with a break for lunch from 11.30am–2pm. Offices also open on Saturday mornings. The best time to get anything done is at the start of the working day. Shops start the day at 8 or 8.30am and close around 6pm, except at hotels and joint ventures, which stay open as late as 9pm. Money exchange outlets are open seven days a week and generally operate long hours.

Note that for tourist sites, ticket sales may stop ½ hour before closing time. Many museums are not open on Monday.

ACCOMMODATION

Luxury hotels abound in Beijing, with many more sprouting up. Bargains don't, largely due to state-set minimums on room rates. Hotels marked 'JV' are joint ventures run by foreign management, which normally means that they offer better service at a higher cost than their state-run counterparts.

Early morning traffic

Great Wall Sheraton

Rates at all but the cheapest hotels are subject to 10–15 percent service surcharge. Hotel published rates for standard rooms are coded as follows:

$$$$$ = US$200 and up
$$$$ = US$150–US$199
$$$ = US$100–US$149
$$ = US$50–US$99
$ = below US$50

BEIJING BAMBOO GARDEN HOTEL (JV)
24 Xiaoshiqiao Lane
Jiugulou Dajie
Tel: 403-2229
Modest and clean rooms that open into a classical-style Chinese garden. The hotel is found just one block from the Drum Tower. $$

BEIJING FRIENDSHIP HOTEL
3 Baishiqiao Road
Tel: 849-8080
Old style state-run hotel in the peaceful northwest corner of town. Located near the universities and the Summer Palace. $

BEIJING HOTEL
33 East Chang'an Avenue
Tel: 513-7766
Old haunt for foreigners, sandwiched between Tiananmen Square and the Wangfujing shopping district. Rooms available in the east building only. One of Beijing's best known hotels. $$$

BEIJING INTERNATIONAL HOTEL
9 Jianguomennei Dajie
Tel: 512-6688
Somewhat dingy standard accommodation, but very well situated for sightseeing and business. Five-minute taxi ride to Tiananmen Square. $$$

CHINA WORLD HOTEL (JV)
1 Jianguomenwai Dajie
Tel: 505-2266
Top of the line service and accommodations, well located for business. Health club with swimming pool, shopping plaza and business centre, plus a variety of Western and Oriental restaurants. Part of a huge complex that includes the China World Trade Centre. $$$$$

FRAGRANT HILLS HOTEL
Fragrant Hills Park
Tel: 259-1166
Sunny modern getaway in the lush hills to the northwest of Beijing, near Summer Palace, but far from the city. Outdoor swimming pool, Chinese and Western restaurants. $$

GREAT WALL SHERATON HOTEL (JV)
East Third Ring Road
Tel: 500-5566
Pleasant American joint venture hotel with swimming pool, numerous lounges and restaurants. Runs well-organized day tours of main Beijing sites. $$$

HILTON HOTEL (JV)
4 Dong Sanhuan Beilu
Tel: 466-2288
Brand new 5-star hotel right off the airport expressway. Posh surroundings and good food. *$$$*

HOTEL NEW OTANI CHANGFUGONG (JV)
26 Jianguomenwai Dajie
Tel: 512-5555
Japanese joint venture with swimming pool and health club. Well located for business in the eastern part of the city. *$$$*

HOLIDAY INN CROWNE PLAZA BEIJING (JV)
48 Wangfujing Dajie
Dengshikou
Tel: 513-3388
Located on a busy shopping street in central Beijing, close to the Forbidden City and other Imperial City sites. Health club and swimming pool. *$$$*

HOTEL BEIJING-TORONTO (JV)
3 Jianguomenwai Dajie
Tel: 500-2266
Friendly 4-star accommodation in eastern Beijing. *$$$*

Jianguo Hotel

JIANGUO HOTEL (JV)
5 Jianguomenwai Dajie
Tel: 500-2233
A favourite for long-term business travellers to the city. Experienced staff and a comfortable atmosphere. Located in eastern Beijing. Good value. *$$*

KEMPINSKI HOTEL
(BEIJING LUFTHANSA CENTRE) (JV)
50 Liangmaqiao Lu
Tel: 465-3388
Shiny new 5-star hotel with the works. Attached to Youyi Shopping City. *$$$$*

Palace Hotel

HOLIDAY INN LIDO HOTEL (JV)
Jiangtai Lu
Tel: 437-6688
A village unto itself catering to short and long-term guests. Indoor/outdoor swimming, tennis courts, business and shopping facilities. Near the airport. *$$*

NOVOTEL (JV)
88 Dengshikou
Tel: 513-8822
Clean, no frills, centrally located. A real bargain for Beijing. *$$*

PEACE HOTEL (JV)
3 Goldfish Lane
Wangfujing
Tel: 512-8833
Unremarkable rooms, centrally located for shopping and Imperial City sights. Lively nightlife in this neighbourhood. *$$$*

PALACE HOTEL (JV)
8 Goldfish Lane
Wangfujing
Tel: 512-8899
Posh 5-star hotel run by the army. Centrally located for shopping and Imperial City sites on a lively downtown alleyway. Restaurants for all palates and designer shopping. *$$$$$*

QIANMEN HOTEL BEIJING
175 Yongan Lu
Tel: 301-6688
Standard accommodations in old outer city, near the Temple of Heaven. Peking opera performances nightly. *$$*

RITAN HOTEL
1 Ritan Road
Jianguomenwai
Tel: 512-5588

Intimate little hotel located inside Ritan Park. Peaceful and reasonably-priced for basic accommodation. $

SARA HOTEL (HUAQIAO DASHA)
2 Wangfujing Dajie
Tel: 513-6666
Comfortable atmosphere and deluxe accommodation in a downtown location. $$$

SHANGRI-LA HOTEL
29 Zizhuyuan Road
Tel: 841-2211
Top-notch accommodation with experienced service staff and friendly surroundings. Located on the western edge of town, but shuttle buses are available. $$$$

Lobby, Shangri-La

SWISSOTEL BEIJING
(HONG KONG MACAU CENTRE) (JV)
Gongrentiyuguan Beilu
Chaoyangmen Beidajie
Tel: 501-2288
New luxury highrise hotel just northwest of main business area. $$$

TRADERS HOTEL
(CHINA WORLD TRADE CENTRE) (JV)
1 Jianguomenwai Dajie
Tel: 505-2277
Good solid service, food and accommodation. Well located for business in the east section of the city. $$$

XIN QIAO HOTEL (JV)
2 Dong Jiaomin Xiang
Dongcheng District
Elegant old-style hotel located in the former Legation Quarter, close to Tiananmen Square. Peaceful and convenient to transportation. $$

HEALTH AND EMERGENCIES

Hygiene/General Health

Tap water should always be boiled before drinking. Some hotels have water purification systems and others provide bottled water and hot water in thermoses. Bottled mineral water and canned soft drinks are available at most tourist sites and on busy streets.

Although they are not necessarily unsafe, it is advisable to avoid ice cream, yoghurt and drinks from large vats. If you buy food from vendors on the street, make sure it is very hot and freshly cooked, and served in clean dishes, preferably disposable. Peel all fruits.

Avoid eateries with dirty utensils or poor food handling practices to avoid contracting hepatitis, which is endemic. And this can't be stressed enough: wash your hands frequently.

Outside the hotels, most toilets are marginal. Carry your own toilet paper wherever you go. Better public toilets sometimes require you to pay a small fee.

The most common complaints of travellers are colds and stomach disorders. Attention to hygiene goes a long way to preventing both. Medicines that may come in handy are Panadol, Lomotil (or Imodium) general antibiotics, Pepto-Bismol and aspirin. The Watson's Drug Store in the Palace Hotel has the widest selection of Western drugs. If you're planning an extended visit to China, consult a physician about vaccinations.

Medical Services

In case of a dire emergency, dial 120 for an ambulance. The best hospital for foreigners is the Sino-Japanese Friendship Hospital (north end of Heping Street, Chaoyang District, Tel: 422-1122). The new International Medical Centre (Beijing Lufthansa Centre, Tel: 465-1561) is an outpatient clinic geared to foreigners.

COMMUNICATIONS AND NEWS

Post

Hotel desks provide the most convenient service for travellers with ordinary letters and parcels. The International Post and

Beijing International Post and Telecommunications office

Telecommunications Office (open daily 8am–7pm) at Yabao Lu, about 300m (327yds) north of the Jianguomen Overpass handles international mail.

Telephone

Beijing's telecommunications network has improved dramatically in recent years. Major hotels have IDD service available in the rooms and smaller hotels normally have business centres with IDD. In the past year, a number of telephone kiosks have sprung up in shopping areas, where you pay cash to the booth attendants for overseas and domestic long distance or local calls. Keep in mind that China's IDD rates are among the highest in the world and that hotels usually add a service charge. If using an AT&T phone card, dial the access number: 10811. Fax and cable services are also widely available in hotels.

Another option is the International Post and Telecommunications Office mentioned under *Post*. Besides long distance

calls, it handles remittances, money orders and telegraphic money transfers. The Long-Distance Telephone Building at Fuxingmennei Dajie (7am–midnight) handles long-distance, conference and pre-booked telephone calls. The Telephone Building on West Chang'an Avenue (open 24 hours) has a complete range of telephone and fax services.

Local calls can be made from booths with attendants and cost 10 fen. Coin-operated phones are often out of order.

Useful Telephone Numbers

(bilingual English and Chinese)
PUBLIC SECURITY BUREAU
Foreigners Section
Tel: 555-486

INTERNATIONAL SOS FIRST AID CENTRE
Tel: 500-3419

Flight Information Telephone Numbers

Capital Airport Information: 456-3604
Air China domestic bookings: 601-3336
Air China international bookings: 601-6667

Media

The English-language *China Daily* reports domestic and foreign news with an official slant. The *China Daily* also publishes *Beijing Weekend*, a tabloid-size weekly that highlights happenings around town and runs feature articles about the city. Both are available at hotels and at the Friendship Store.

The *International Herald Tribune, Asian Wall Street Journal*, Hong Kong newspapers and major international news magazines are available at the same locations.

Most major hotels now offer CNN's 24-hour programming. Star TV from Hong Kong and some Japanese programming is also widely available. China Central Television carries English language news at 10.30pm. Local programmes and most imported programmes are broadcast in Chinese. Local radio broadcasts in English and other languages can be heard on 12.51AM and 91.55FM.

USEFUL INFORMATION

Tourist Information
The Beijing Tourism Administration has a new hotline for emergencies and information: 513-0828. The English spoken at the other end is not perfect (to put it kindly) but if you're away from your hotel, it's worth a try. Most hotels have their own travel agencies for arranging cars and tours. Make good use of the information desk or concierge at your hotel to check on events and opening and closing times. It never hurts to call ahead.

There are several English language publications available in hotels which feature ongoing events in the city. The *China Daily* carries entertainment listings, as does *Travel China*, a bi-weekly and *Welcome to China*, a quarterly.

For information on travel elsewhere in China, your best bet is to check with the travel agency in your hotel. Or contact China International Travel Service (CITS) at Tel: 601-3089. This is China's main state-run tourism bureau, with branch offices throughout the country.

LANGUAGE

Large hotels usually have plenty of English speaking workers to handle needs within the hotel and help arrange logistics for travel and tours. Outside, you'll find a lot of people who speak a little English, but few who speak a lot. Interpreters of English, French, Japanese, Italian, German and Spanish can be employed through CITS. Price is negotiable depending on the size of the group. The list below and the Chinese character list of key places mentioned in this guide on the following pages will help you communicate with taxi drivers.

USEFUL PHRASES

Hello/ How are you?	Ni Hao?
Goodbye	Zai jian
Thank You	Xie xie
I'm sorry/ Excuse me	Dui bu qi
No problem	Mei you wen ti
How much does it cost?	Duo shao qian
Wait a moment	Deng yi xia
No, don't have	Mei you
It doesn't matter	Mei you guan xi
I want	Wo yao
Good	Hao
Bad	Bu hao
Not possible	Bu xing
restaurant	fan dian
taxi	chu zu qi che
telephone	dian hua
hotel	bin guan
train	huo che
airplane	fei ji
toilet	ce suo
north	bei
south	nan
east	dong
west	xi
middle	zhong
street	jie
avenue	dajie
road	lu
gate	men
outside	wai
inside	nei
one	yi
two	er
three	san
four	si
five	wu
six	liu
seven	qi
eight	ba
nine	jiu
ten	shi

Altar to the Earth Park (*Ditan Gongyuan*)	地坛公园
Ancient Culture Street	古文化街
Arthur M. Sakler Gallery of Art and Archaeology at Peking University	北京大学亚瑟·姆·赛克勒考古与艺术博物馆
Beidaihe	北戴河
Guesthouse for Diplomatic Missions	北戴河外交人员宾馆
Beihai Park (*Beihai Gongyuan*)	北海公园
Beijing Great Wall Shooting Range	北京长城射击场
Beijing Hotel	北京饭店
Bell Tower (*Gulou*)	钟楼
Bishushanzhuang Summer Residence	避暑山庄
Chang Ling	长陵
Chang'an Jie (Avenue of Eternal Peace)	长安街
Chengde	承德
Chengde Guesthouse for Diplomatic Missions	承德外交人员宾馆
Club Peak	磬锤峰
Confucius Temple (*Kong Miao*)	孔庙
Confucian Tradition Restaurant	孔膳饭庄
Dashalar	大栅栏
De Ling	德陵
Ding Ling	定陵
Drum Tower (*Gulou*)	鼓楼
Fangshan Restaurant	仿膳饭庄
Forbidden City/Palace Museum (*Gugong*)	故宫
Five Dragon Pavilion (*Wulongting*)	五龙亭
Foreign Legation Quarter	外国租界区
Fragrant Hills Hotel (*Xiangshan Fandian*)	香山饭店
Fragrant Hills Park (*Xiangshan Gongyuan*)	香山公园
Friendship Store	友谊商店
Front Lake (*Qianhai*)	前海
Goubuli Baozi Restaurant	狗不理包子铺
Great Hall of the People	人民大会堂
Great Red Gate (*Dagongmen*)	大红门
Great Wall (at Mutianyu)/ (*Wanlichangcheng*)	万里长城（慕田峪）
Hall of Abstinence (*Zhaigong*)	斋宫
Hall of Prayer for Good Harvest (*Qi'niandian*)	祈年殿
Hongqiao Farmers' Market (*Hongqiao Nongmao Sichang*)	红桥农贸市场
Hyatt Tianjin Hotel	天津凯悦饭店
Imperial Vault of Heaven (*Huangqiong Yu*)	皇穹宇
Jade Island (*Qiong Dao*)	琼岛
Jewelry Street (*Zhubaoshi Jie*)	珠宝石街
Jingshan Park (*Jingshan Gongyuan*)	景山公园
Jingshan Hotel	金山宾馆
Lama Temple (*Yonghegong*)	雍和宫
Liberation Bridge (*Jiefang Qiao*)	解放桥
Little Western Heaven (*Xiaoxitian*)	小西天
Liulichang	琉璃厂
Liyueyuan Garden	李月园
Longevity Hill (*Wanshou Shan*)	万寿山

Lotus Flower Market	荷花市场
Mao Zedong Mausoleum	毛主席纪念堂
Marco Polo Bridge (*Lugouqiao*)	芦沟桥
McDonald's	麦当劳
Monument to the Heroes of the People	人民英雄纪念碑
Museum of Chinese History and Revolution	中国革命历史博物馆
Natural History Museum	自然历史博物馆
Neiliansheng Shoe Store	内联升
Number Two Department Store	第二百货商店
Ox Street Mosque (*Niu Jie Qingzhen Si*)	牛街清真寺
Palace Hotel (*Wangfu Fandian*)	王府饭店
Puning Temple (Universal Peace Temple)	普宁寺
Pule Temple (Universal Happiness Temple)	普乐寺
Putuozhongsheng	普陀寺　乘之庙
Qianmen	前门
Qianmen Women's Clothing Store	前门妇女服装店
Rear Lake/Houhai	后海
Restaurant for Foreign Diplomatic Missions	外交人员大酒家
Rongbaozhai Shop	荣宝斋
Round Mound	圆丘
Ruifuxiang Silk and Cotton Fabric Store	瑞蚨祥绸布店
Silk Alley (*Xiushui Shichang*)	秀水市场
Spectacles Lake (*Yanjinghu*)	眼镜湖
Summer Palace (*Yiheyuan*)	颐和园
Suzhou Street (*Suzhou Jie*)	苏州街
Temple of Clarity (*Zhaomiao*)	昭庙
Temple of Heaven (*Tiantan*)	天坛公园
Temple of the Azure Clouds (*Biyunsi*)	碧云寺
Temple of the Source of the Law (*Fayuansi*)	法源寺
Tiananmen	天安门
Tiananmen Square	天安门广场
Tianqiao Paradise Teahouse/	天桥乐茶馆
Tianqiao Le Chaguan	
Tongrentang Traditional Medicine Shop	同仁堂
Underground City	地下城
Wangfujing Street	王府井大街
Wanping	宛平
Way of the Spirit (*Shendao*)	神道
White Dagoba (*Baita*)	白塔
Wumen	午门
Xizhimen Bird Market	西直门鸟市场
Xumifushou Temple	须弥福寿之庙
(Sumera Happiness and Longevity Temple)	
Xumilingjing Buddhist Temple	须弥灵境址
Yabao Market (*Yabao Shichang*)	压宝市场
Yert Holiday Inn	蒙古包度假村
Yunshan Hotel	云山饭店
Zhang Yiyuan Tea Shop	张一圆茶庄
Zhengyangmen/Qianmen	正阳门
Zhongnanhai	中南海
Zhongshan Park (*Zhongshan Gongyuan*)	中山公园

Index

Cover	DJ Heaton/Apa Photo
Back Cover	Erhard Pansegrau
Photography	Kari Huus *and*
Pages 8/9, 25T, 26, 38B, 58B, 70, 74B	Patrick Lucero
75B, 82T, 84, 87, 88B	
2/3, 13, 15, 16T, 16B, 18T	Manfred Morgenstern
31T, 85	Erhard Pansegrau
57B	Machtelb Stikvoort
76T, 76B, 77	Xinhua News Agency
Desktop Operator	Caroline Low
Handwriting	V. Barl
Cover Design	Klaus Geisler
Cartography	Berndtson & Berndtson

North America	Corsica	Middle East and Africa
Atlanta	**C**orsica	**I**stanbul
Boston	Costa Blanca	**K**enya
British Coumbia	Costa Brava	**M**aldives
Florida	Cote d'Azur	Morocco
Florida Keys	Crete	**S**eychelles
Hawaii	**D**enmark	Tunisia
Miami	**F**lorence	Turkish Coast
Montreal	**G**ran Canaria	**Asia/Pacific**
New York City	**H**ungary	**B**ali
North California	**I**biza	Bali Birdwalks
Quebec	Ireland	Bangkok
San Francisco	**L**isbon	Beijing
South California	Loire Valley	Bhutan
Toronto	London	**C**anton
Latin America and	**M**adrid	Chiang Mai
The Caribbean	Mallorca	**F**iji
Bahamas	Malta	**H**ong Kong
Baja	Marbella	**J**akarta
Belize	Milan	**K**athmandu,
Bermuda	Moscow	Bikes & Hikes
Jamaica	Munich	Kuala Lumpur
Mexico City	**O**slo/Bergen	**M**acau
Puerto Rico	**P**aris	Malacca
US Virgin Islands	Prague	**N**epal
Yucatan Peninsula	Provence	New Delhi
Europe	**R**hodes	New Zealand
Aegean Islands	Rome	**P**enang
Algarve	**S**ardinia	Phuket
Alsace	Scotland	**S**abah
Athens	Seville	Sikkim
Barcelona	Sicily	Singapore
Bavaria	Southeast England	Sri Lanka
Berlin	St Petersburg	Sydney
Brittany	**T**enerife	**T**hailand
Brussels	Tuscany	Tibet
Budapest	**V**enice	**Y**ogyakarta
	Vienna	

● ●

United States: **Houghton Mifflin Company, Boston MA 02108**
Tel: (800) 2253362 Fax: (800) 4589501

Canada: **Thomas Allen & Son, 390 Steelcase Road East**
Markham, Ontario L3R 1G2
Tel: (416) 4759126 Fax: (416) 4756747

Great Britain: **GeoCenter UK, Hampshire RG22 4BJ**
Tel: (256) 817987 Fax: (256) 817988

Worldwide: **Höfer Communications Singapore 2262**
Tel: (65) 8612755 Fax: (65) 8616438

66 I was first drawn to the Insight Guides by the excellent "Nepal" volume. I can think of no book which so effectively captures the essence of a country. Out of these pages leaped the Nepal I know – the captivating charm of a people and their culture. I've since discovered and enjoyed the entire Insight Guide Series. Each volume deals with a country or city in the same sensitive depth, which is nowhere more evident than in the superb photography. **99**

Sir Edmund Hillary

INSIGHT GUIDES

COLORSET NUMBERS

You'll find the colorset number on the spine of each Insight Guide.